I wish Dick Benson had written this book fifty years ago. Truly, this is a book that belongs on every copywriter's bookshelf, and one that is worth careful reading and rereading. And, best of all, it is fun!
Walter Weintz, copywriter

Here's an extraordinary guarantee: If Benson's great book doesn't make money for you, return it to me, with your canceled check, for a full refund.
Martin Edelston, Boardroom Reports, Inc.

Dick Benson is a giant of direct mail and his new book is a landmark in the literature of that exciting and demanding business. Ignore it at your own peril.
Jonah Gitlitz, President, Direct Marketing Association

Dick Benson is a man with a remarkable history of accomplishment and with this book he has recorded his direct-mail heritage: page after page of breakthrough direct-mail marketing. Each page, each idea compounds upon each of the others to create resoundingly successful direct mail.
Polly Jensen, General Chairman, 1988 Chicago/Midwest Direct Marketing Days

From wine to grapefruit, magazines to Bibles, cameras to polar excursions, Dick Benson has sold them all and most of them successfully. This book is as much fun to read as it is easy to learn from. It is an extraordinary gift to the direct-mail business from one of the men who helped invent it.
Thomas O. Ryder, President, American Express Publishing Corp.

The incomparable Dick Benson...brilliantly shares his first forty years as counsellor to the great and famous in publishing, mail order and retailing. You'll be inspired to take another look at your own methods, copy, offers, business plan, when reading what may well be the most important marketing text of the century.
Henry R. "Pete" Hoke, Jr, Direct Marketing magazine

SECRETS
OF SUCCESSFUL
DIRECT MAIL

SECRETS
OF SUCCESSFUL
DIRECT MAIL

Richard V. Benson

NTC Business Books
a division of *NTC Publishing Group* • Lincolnwood, Illinois USA

This edition first published in 1989 by NTC Business Books,
a division of NTC Publishing Group,
4255 West Touhy Avenue,
Lincolnwood (Chicago), Illinois 60646-1975 U.S.A.
Manufactured in the United States of America.
Library of Congress Catalog Card Number: 88-62906

9 0 BC 9 8 7 6 5 4 3 2 1

*To Evelyn, my wife and partner for forty years,
and to my daughter, Helen Mullen,
the best business partner I ever had.*

CONTENTS

FOREWORD

I hope you've bought this book or at least gone to the trouble of stealing it, because it's worth at least that. Should you have the further good sense to read it and take it to heart, your fortunes in direct-mail marketing promise to improve dramatically. It is the equivalent of a doctoral-level course in how to make a great deal of money legitimately through the mail, and may well be the most valuable book ever written on the subject.

I confess I'm partial. I've known Dick Benson for 20 years, worked for him, learned from him, contributed to some of the projects he ranks among his successes, failed him on some others and, I am sure, disappointed him on many occasions. He has enriched my work and my life; it is a source of great and continuing reassurance to me not only that he does exist, but that he can exist—and prosper—in a world ruled by hype. For Dick Benson is the very antithesis of hype; he is the ultimate counter-B.S. artist, that rarest of birds, a man who really is what he appears to be. He is man without artifice, a man who says what he thinks regardless of how costly that may be to him, a man who is direct, blunt, to the point, brutally frank, sometimes abrasive, ill-inclined to suffer fools gladly or embellish his judgments with diplomatic flourishes.

His brusqueness sometimes puts off clients and prospective clients. But the smart ones understand it and shrug it off, because they have discovered a crucial underlying truth about Dick Benson: he is almost always right. Right more often, indeed, than he would have you believe in this book, for he talks as freely about his failures as he does about his successes. How like him, I thought when I read it. How like him to be as unsparing of himself as he is of misguided clients. And how like him to write the book himself—no ghost writers, no editing for style (only for clarity in a few spots), no self-aggrandizement or puffery, no punches pulled for fear of offending.

It is his story, told by him in his own words, in his own inimitable style. It sounds just like him. The way he writes is the way he speaks—clear, incisive, uncluttered, disciplined, sometimes acerbic, sometimes masterfully understated, brisk, fast-paced, lively. There is no patina to dull the brilliance or impact of what he says. The book is almost all meat, a triumph of content and meaning over verbiage. Dick Benson is not one to waste words, in life or in print. And so there's hardly a page that doesn't contain some insight, idea or observation that can be worth a small fortune (often a large one) to you. I was struck not only by how much I'd forgotten but by how much I never knew in the first place.

I've been in this business for 30 years and I've worked with and known well some of the brightest and most effective direct-mail marketers of our time. But Dick Benson is in a class by himself. He is an authentic genius (I'd guess his I.Q. must be off the scale) who happens to have devoted his time, energy and passion to direct-mail marketing because he loves it, loves the challenge, loves the accountability. It is a perfect match of man and work; he has become the best (arguably the best ever) in a line of endeavor where the results are precisely measurable in dollars. He has chosen to live on Skidaway Island off the coast of Georgia, but as long as his clients can count the money his advice brings in for them, he could live on Mars (as long there were a telephone hook-up). What's more—and this is a most persuasive accolade—he has become a rich man by taking his own advice. If I had to create a truly high-stakes mailing—say, I'd be shot if it didn't work—I'd go to Dick Benson.

Some of the best and most absorbing years of my working life were those I spent connected with Benson, Stagg & Associates, the firm founded by Dick Benson (who subsequently took on the late Christopher Stagg as a creative head and second-in-command). I was a freelance copy-writer for Benson, Stagg for a while, then came aboard as a creative director at their invitation. Benson, Stagg enjoyed a reputation at the time as the top direct-mail marketing agency in New York (and therefore the world), while almost all of its work was farmed out to a list of freelance copy-writers and designers that reads today like a "who's who." Benson, Stagg functioned as a sort of client's agent, buying the best and most appropriate creative work for a particular client or project. Dick Benson would become involved in creative decisions only when he thought something was wrong, and he was usually right; his seldom-exercised creative judgment was uncanny, right on target. Other than that, he relied on our creative judgment, respected and valued our work. The system functioned very well because it worked well for the clients. It is a tribute to the organization Dick Benson put together that the firm's name is still known—and that the firm's accomplishments and the quality of its work have yet to be surpassed. I don't think the staff—including secretaries and office boys—ever exceeded 14 or so; Dick Benson had little enthusiasm for empire building.

I did a lot of growing at Benson, Stagg. I think we all did; Dick Benson is a marvelous teacher. It was an exciting time. Benson, Stagg was right at the center of things in an era when direct-mail marketing was just beginning to take flight. And so I was greatly saddened to see it all come to an end, which it more or less did when the company was sold to a conglomerate. I moved to Los Angeles to open a West Coast office for Benson, Stagg; Dick Benson and Chris Stagg had an irreparable falling out (especially painful for me, because they both were my friends); Dick resigned from the firm and I soon discovered that I was neither happy nor very good at running an office. I resigned and went back to freelancing and Benson, Stagg vanished a few months later in a corporate reshuffle.

I learned more from Dick Benson than I can ever imaginably repay; I suspect most of his clients feel the same way. But this—and the vast sums he has helped so many clients earn—are only part of his legacy. This bright, creative, brusque, introverted, sometimes difficult, sometimes shy, sometimes awkward man is one of the most honest, decent and generous-spirited people I've ever known. What you keep hearing from those who know Dick, people who have worked for and with him, clients past and present, is not how successful they've become by following his advice; that's taken for granted. What you keep hearing, instead, is the affection they feel for him. In case you missed it, that is also what you are hearing from me. Dick Benson is a very special man, and it is my great good fortune to count him among my friends.

In a sense, this book is a series of sessions with Dick Benson, an opportunity of inestimable value in and of itself. But is is still at one remove from the real thing. If I can offer a recommendation to anyone who wishes to succeed in direct-mail marketing, it is to head for Skidaway Island, pay Dick Benson whatever he asks—and *listen*.

Hank Burnett
Santa Barbara, California
August 9, 1987

PREFACE

Introducing a very *direct* mail man . . .

> The single best editor, marketer, genius I've ever met is Richard V. Benson. Temperamental, short-tempered, Dick has a boredom threshold that starts one-tenth of an inch off the floor. He is also capable of stunning insights into a client's direct-marketing problems. After all, Dick was the only human in our world who believed that $500,000 could be raised for the Admiral Byrd transpolar expedition by spending just $5,000. (He was wrong. Six hundred thousand dollars was raised for the same $5,000.)

Freelance writer Chris Stagg said it, and dozens of America's most successful direct marketers agree. They risked his bark and his bite because the rewards were so great. They listened to Dick, they learned from Dick, they followed Dick's advice all the way to the top of their different specialities.

And they are still doing it today.

Dick Benson's genius is unique. He can crunch numbers faster than most computers. But just as quickly, he can take demographics and turn the numbers into living, breathing human beings a marketer can reach—and sell.

Who is this man, this genius, this mentor and consultant to the stars of direct-mail advertising?

A child of the Depression. A Horatio Alger story. A man,

successful beyond his own wildest dreams, who is more convinced than ever that the American Dream can come true.

He was born in Panama in 1921, the only child of American parents. Three years later, a flood wiped out the family banana plantation. His father took his wife and son to New York and promptly abandoned them. Dick's mother struggled and struggled, but in 1926, when he was five, she had to send him to a foster home in eastern Maryland. Like many Depression kids, he often went hungry. But at least he didn't starve.

When he was 11 years old, his mother took him away from the home and settled in Washington, D.C. He worked at every job a youngster could find in those dark years, but managed to graduate from high school—in the bottom quarter of his class.

Despite the dire warnings of teachers who said he was too dumb for college, he entered Maryland University and worked his way through as a department store clerk, construction laborer, doorman and streetcar conductor. One job paid 25 cents an hour. Another at least gave him eating money, but he had to work 48 hours a week and join the union to earn the $12 that kept him going. He certainly learned the value of money—a lesson he is still teaching today.

Finishing college early with a degree in political science—and again in the bottom quarter of his class—he spent World War II as a cryptanalyst for the U.S. Navy Department, controller of the French Military Mission and foreign-service clerk in the U.S. Embassy in Chungking.

But that was as close as he ever got to realizing his schoolboy dream of becoming a career diplomat. He had a second, conflicting dream. Like Horatio Alger, he wanted to make a million dollars, and foreign service was no way to do it. So after the war, he tried accounting, selling and market research. He tried everything! And then, one brilliantly sunny day in August, 1947, he found himself—and his future. He fell into a job as circulation-business manager at Time-Life International, where he discovered circulation-promotion and the direct mail world he loves.

After Time, he became general manager of *Onmibook*, publisher-owner of *Scarab* magazine, assistant to the treasurer of Merganthaler Linotype, circulation director of *Field & Stream*, associate publisher of *World* magazine, and vice president for circulation of the American Heritage Publishing Company, where his colossal creativity and pure cussedness became an industry legend.

At the age of 40, Richard V. Benson had invented more direct-mail "rules," taught more people about common sense in advertising and sold more subscriptions for his employers than any man since. But he still hadn't made the elusive million dollars for himself. So in 1961, he left American Heritage to become a full-time consultant on his own.

As American Heritage president James Parton said:

> I found it [Benson's departure] a bitter pill to swallow because I realized that it would be literally impossible to replace his entrepreneurial genius. Never after that did American Heritage Publishing Company have the same degree of promotional flair and ingenuity.

Jim Parton is only one of the legendary figures you will meet in this book. You will work with Dick Benson alongside Bert Garmise, Walter Weintz, Max Geffen, Bruce Catton, Jerry Hardy, Lester Wunderman, David Ogilvy, Martin Baier, Luther Breck, Dick Leventer, Emory Cunningham, George Hirsch, Clay Felker, Ed Mayer, Jim Prendergast, John Suhler, Nina Link, Bill Capps, Bob Krefting, Alan Drey, Richard Viguerie, Frank Schultz, Lester Suhler, Julian Haydon, Rodney Friedman and others.

You'll sit in on creative sessions with America's top freelance copywriters and art directors: Frank Johnson, Hank Burnett, Bob Jones, Jack Walsh, Bill Jayme, Richard Browner, Dick Archer, Chris Stagg, Todd Weintz, Linda Wells, Harry Walsh, Tom McCormick, Henry Cowen, Herschel Lewis, Irwin Glusker and Bob Fisler. You'll learn—step-by-step and package component-by-component—Dick Benson's techniques for creating a winner.

You'll read about his successes—and failures—in marketing *American Heritage,* the Culinary Society, Time-Life Books, the clients of Ogilvy & Mather, the *New Republic,* Old American Insurance, the Internal Revenue Service, Breck's, the Admiral Byrd Society, *Encyclopaedia Britannica,* the *Weekly Reader,* Insurance Company of North America, Cresta Blanca, *Redbook, Psychology Today, Southern Living,* the *Wall Street Journal,* the Tourist Commission of Spain, McGraw-Hill, the *Christian Science Monitor, U.S. News & World Report, Harper's* magazine, 3M Company, Children's Television Workshop, the *Contest News-Letter,* Southern Landmarks, Historical Times Plates, the Hearst Corporation, Johnson & Johnson, Yield House, Richard Viguerie Company, Goodbee Pecans, *Smithsonian,* Knapp Publishing Company, the *University of California, Berkeley Wellness Letter* and R.L. Polk, with its diversity of clients.

Secrets of Successful Direct Mail is the story of countless dreams-come-true—and of the man who made them happen. It is the story of a grumpy genius who made millions for other people before he made that first million for himself.

> *Linda Wells*
> *London, England*
> *July 15, 1987*

INTRODUCTION

This is a book about direct marketing by mail—not space, not radio, not TV, but mail and mail only. I have been a specialist in the mail marketing of magazine subscriptions, but my experience also includes the sale of books, one-shot merchandise and insurance, as well as catalogs and fund raising.

More testing is done by magazine publishers selling subscriptions than is done by the rest of the industry because of the enormous volume of mail and the relatively low unit price of magazines. As a result, the big breakthroughs in mail tend to come from the magazine publishers.

My first exposure to direct mail came in 1947, when I went to work at Time Inc. In those days, Time Inc. was one of the very major volume mailers and was a leader in the successful use of mail.

The following is a chronicle of my successes and failures beginning in 1954 with my tenure at American Heritage Publishing Company, where I was a vice president. In 1961, I became a consultant and since then I have worked with more than 100 clients.

When I became a direct-mail consultant I was aware of only three other consultants. Bert Garmise had been circulation director of the *Saturday Review* and as a consultant headed a company where he acted as the circulation department for some 20 magazines. I had been his client when I was associate publisher at *World* magazine as well as when I was circulation director of *Field & Stream*. Walter Weintz, the creative giant, who had been circulation director of *Reader's Digest*, was a freelance writer and consultant. Bill Steiner, a former circulation manager, was the third and he was also a freelance writer and consultant.

In the ensuing years, the direct-mail industry has exploded and nowhere is this better exemplified than in the number of consultants in the field. It seems to me there are now hundreds.

For the past ten years I have also been a publisher. *Contest News-Letter*, which I sold to *McCall's* in 1986, was the largest paid-subscription newsletter in the United States, with a circulation of 750,000. The *University of California, Berkeley, Wellness Letter*, first published in 1984, has a current subscription base of 500,000 and is the second largest newsletter.

The book leads off with my 31 rules of thumb, rules that I believe to prevail generally in all mail. Following this is my experience at *American Heritage* and client case histories that illustrate many of my rules of thumb.

Various aspects of selling by direct mail are then detailed. Finally, I will explain my present view of direct mail.

1
BENSON'S
RULES
OF
THUMB

n defense of these prejudices: I have a lot of scar tissue backing up these principles. I offer them to you with this qualifier: They work for me.

1. A two-time buyer is twice as likely to buy as a one-time buyer. Most of the experts I know who issue catalogs, handle circulation for publications or raise funds by mail know this to be true.
2. The same product sold at different prices will result in the same net income per thousand mailed.
3. Sweepstakes will improve results by 50% or more.
4. A credit or bill-me offer will improve results by 50% or more.
5. Tokens or stickers always improve results.
6. Memberships renew better than plain subscriptions by 10% or more.

7. "Department store" pricing always pays except for membership offers.
8. You can never sell two things at once.
9. Self-mailers almost never work.
10. The more believable a special offer, the more likely its success.
11. The addition of installment payments for an item over $15 will increase results by 15%.
12. Dollar for dollar, premiums are better incentives than cash discounts.
13. Adding elements to a mailing package, even though obviously adding cost, is more likely to pay out than cheapening the package.
14. For magazines a "soft" offer ("Try a complimentary copy at our risk") is better than a hard offer (cash or "bill me").
15. A Yes-No option will increase orders.
16. "FREE" is a magic word.
17. Two premiums are frequently better than one.
18. Long copy is better than short copy.
19. Personalized letters work better to house lists (those who have bought or subscribed before) than to "cold" lists.
20. Brochures and letters should stand alone and each of them should contain all the information.
21. Direct mail should be scrupulously honest.
22. Subscriptions sold at half-price for at least eight months will convert at renewal time just as strongly as subscriptions sold for a full year at full price.
23. Lists are the most important ingredient to the success of a promotional mailing.
24. The offer is the second most important ingredient of direct mail.
25. Letters should look and feel like letters.
26. An exclusive reduced price to a house list will more than pay its way.
27. To predict final results from a promotion, you can assume you will always receive as many

more orders as you've received in the past week. This projection will generally be valid beginning with the second week's orders and continuing thereafter.

28. A follow-up mailing dropped two weeks after the first mailing will pull 50% of the original response.

29. An incentive to pay cash when you offer both cash and credit options reduces net response.

30. Test-mailing packages are best when they come from independent creative sources.

31. Offers of subscriptions using two terms (i.e., eight months, 16 months) will pull more money… but 10% fewer orders.

Nothing works all the time, but ignore any of these rules at your own peril.

2
WHAT DOES
A
CONSULTANT
DO?

Atruism: What a consultant does is most often shaped by the needs of the client.

My basic perception of my role is to improve the efficiency of the client's direct marketing and to provide solutions to direct-mail problems. Beyond my direct marketing expertise, I am often involved in personnel, research and development, and business life cycles.

In my case, I expect my clients to treat me as a vice president of their company. It is impossible to be even reasonably competent as a consultant if the client is not completely open about his business.

In addition to bringing new ideas to the client as well as a knowledge of what things are currently working or are testworthy, the consultant frequently is a backup or nay-sayer to the client's instincts. Many times the consultant picks up a problem off the floor where it has been put aside for one reason or another and insists the client face up to it and make a decision.

It has always been my policy to give a client direct advice to the best of my ability without regard to whether it was what the client wanted to hear. My advice hasn't always been right, but it was always what I thought was best.

In my view, a consultant is a consultant, not a hands-on employee. In general my clients visit with me for a day or more three or four times a year. Generally speaking this is adequate since something needs to happen between visits so that there will be new information on which to base advice on next steps or new directions.

In between personal visits, there are telephone calls (very frequent with some) to handle any day-to-day questions. Many of my clients keep me updated by copying me with their internal reports. The clients for whom I do the best work are the clients who have done their homework and are well prepared when they see me.

As a general rule I am not involved in production—though if asked I will recommend suppliers. The same is true for copy. Many times I will give my personal briefing to a copywriter. I do not generate reports, but I am regularly involved in the analysis and interpretation of results.

In the past 15 years or more, I have rarely had a contract with a client, which meant if he didn't like my advice he could fire me the same day. I have been fired on short notice and some of those times are included in the following stories. The great benefit of this method of doing business is that it works both ways so that if I didn't think the client listened to me or if I didn't like the client's methods of doing business, I could resign without notice. In fact, I have resigned from as many clients, and with much less tenure on average, as I have had fire me. (I'm not sure that's cause for pride, but it has made me feel good.)

Before we go on to specific marketing stories, let me mention three items that have played a major part in my thinking.

1. As a child of the Depression, I learned the importance of value, which has contributed to my reputation as a "deal man."
2. In college, I took a course in practical algebra, which taught me to analyze the problem, to find what was the right question. So often we

sit in meetings discussing the right answers to the wrong questions. I think it was this course that enabled me to develop the ability to get to the heart of a problem.

3. A book from the Harvard University Press entitled *Make or Buy* converted me to a philosophy of "make only that to which you bring a unique quality and buy everything else around the corner."

3
THE
AMERICAN
HERITAGE
STORY

I want to share some of the hits and misses I've enjoyed—and hated. I have been very fortunate: I've worked with some of the true giants of direct mail. For example:

In 1953, with the help of Bob Straus—a very fine gentleman who with Victor Knauth and Max Geffen owned *Omnibook* magazine—I became associate publisher of *World* magazine, with the duties of general manager and circulation director.

Bob introduced me to James Parton, who, with Joseph Thorndike and Oliver Jenson, operated a magazine consulting firm. *World* was one of their clients. Thorndike, Jenson and Parton all had had major careers at Time Inc. Joe Thorndike was the original editor of *Life*. Oliver Jenson had been an editor at *Life*. Jim Parton had started as a writer for *Time* upon graduation from Harvard; his last assignment for *Time* had been to investigate the idea of creating a new newspaper in Los Angeles by merging a number of "pennysavers." Time Inc. dropped the idea, but Jim, with other backing, had gone on to do it. The idea for a new paper didn't work, and the project was terminated.

World didn't have a clear editorial focus or "umbrella" to attract a loyal group of subscribers. It had operated in the red during the seven years of its existence despite our efforts to find a new, viable editorial format. We mailed a number of test circulation promotion packages containing different editorial promises to see what might attract a larger audience. We failed. At my behest, we closed the publication down at the end of June 1954—only six months after I joined the company.

(I always have held the opinion that in our capitalist society a publication isn't worth doing if, after a fair chance, the public won't support it to at least a break-even point.)

THE FOUNDING OF *AMERICAN HERITAGE*

Jim Parton had begun negotiating the purchase of the *Magazine of Wall Street.* During this same period, the Association for American History came to the Thorndike, Jenson and Parton partnership with *American Heritage,* a quarterly magazine they had been publishing.

As I recall, the Association was worried. The annual expense budget for *American Heritage* had grown to $54,000 and the financial responsibility was too large for the Association.

Courtland Canby, whose father, Vincent Canby, was a member of the selection board of the Book-of-the-Month Club, had tested a bimonthly magazine called *History.* *History* was to be hard-covered, like a book. Harry Sherman, the founder and brilliant mind behind the Book-of-the-Month Club, had supervised *History's* test mailing and felt it was a success.

Despite this, Courtland Canby hadn't been able to get the financing he needed to start publishing.

Parton conceived the idea of marrying the editorial, particularly the pictorial, coverage of *American Heritage* with the editorial and hard cover of *History.* In addition, he wanted to change the quarterly *American Heritage* to the bimonthly concept of *History.*

(A parenthetical comment: There has never been an economically successful quarterly magazine in the entire history of publishing in the United States.)

When I examined the numbers on the *History* test, I felt success was possible. So I encouraged Parton to go ahead with his idea. Parton put together a business plan calling for raising capital of $200,000 to publish *American Heritage*.

Jim Parton was able to attract investors such as Marshall Field; James Sachs of the Wall Street family; Robert Straus of the Macy fortune; Roger Phillips, whose grandfather had discovered and developed gas in Pennsylvania; General Stackpole, a publisher in Pennsylvania; and several other important people. Even with all these, he had commitments for only $38,000. Jim showed his faith by taking a $12,000 mortgage on a house he owned in Vermont.

The company was started July 1, 1954. I well remember Jim opening the bank account with the $50,000 he had raised.

Jim Parton was and is the most able man I have ever worked for. He had been an editorial writer and a promotion copywriter at *Time* and was the best promotion copywriter I have ever known.

THE MASTER OF THE "SECOND SALE"

In my opinion direct mail is the business of the "second sale," and Jim is the master of the second sale.

The second sale for a publication is the conversion or renewal order. The importance of selling the subscriber a second time is that after this renewal he's twice as likely to resubscribe as he would be if he'd bought only once.

Jim likened the second sale to a carnival. After you've entered the tent and seen the girls dance, the pitchman tells you: "You ain't seen nothin' yet. For just one more quarter you can go into the next tent, where the girls dance without any clothes on." Jim knows how to wrap his arms around the customers, love them and induce them to buy again.

Jim Parton taught me two selling lessons I've always tried to keep in mind: Never tell the customer something that isn't true. If you mess up in your service, admit it forthrightly and do whatever you can to fix it.

THE "A" TEAM AT *AMERICAN HERITAGE*

Jim Parton gathered together a remarkable group of people to start *American Heritage*:

Himself;

Joe Thorndike, his partner;

Oliver Jenson, his partner;

Bruce Catton, the Civil War historian and author, as editor;

Irwin Glusker, former art director of *Life*, as art director;

Frank Johnson, promotion director of *Fortune*, as promotion director;

George Breitkreuz as comptroller;

and Dick Benson. I was the circulation director.

Bruce Catton, Oliver Jenson and I increased the $50,000 capital by investing $14,000. My share came from borrowing against my life insurance.

LAUNCHING *AMERICAN HERITAGE*

Today, it seems incredible to me that we could successfully launch a magazine for only $64,000; in fact, we borrowed no money until five years later, when we started *Horizon* magazine and published our first major book, *Great Historic Places*.

Contrast this with today. In my opinion, testing a new magazine or product requires a minimum 150,000-piece mail-drop, costing $90,000 to $100,000. (Without a house list I won't consider a smaller test.)

A "cash only" effort at a subscription price of $12—a very

high price in those days—to the previous subscribers of *American Heritage* provided the money for launch mailing. The print order for our first issue was 60,000 copies. It sold out.

American Heritage was very plush, with a great deal of four-color art. It was printed on sheet-fed presses; this was before the day of four-color web presses. One of the big surprises to us was that the 60,000 copies went through the bindery as 20 separate orders of 3,000 each—the ultimate economic unit for binding a book.

Under postal law at the time, because *American Heritage* was hard-covered it had to mail at book rate. This made it much more expensive to mail than an ordinary magazine.

Jim Parton was smart enough to go to Congress and arrange for a bill to be put through changing the law to define a magazine as an editorial product and not a physical one. We were then able to mail *American Heritage* at the reduced second-class postal rate.

For me, this was a great lesson in our American democracy.

SOME FIRSTS

During the mid-1950s, direct mail—including everything—generally cost about $60 per thousand pieces. Postage was $10 and lists were $15.

Except for some catalog sheets, there were no four-color brochures in mass mail. The creative people at *American Heritage* (Jim Parton, Irwin Glusker, Frank Johnson) invented the modern four-color brochure. Jim Parton established a rule that brochures and letters should each stand alone (i.e., both should contain all the facts as well as the offer). Irwin Glusker, our art director, decided that brochures should "track" and each fold should open in a logical progression.

American Heritage was spending $110 per thousand instead of the more normal $60 because we were the first to understand that cost per order was what mattered, not cost per thousand. This was a great step forward. I'm not at all sure we understood the importance of it at the time.

Along the way, *American Heritage* introduced pictorial envelopes. A four-color picture covered the poster side, and the address was on the flap side. An interesting sidelight was that several firms introduced envelopes with addressing on the flap side and left the poster side blank. They believed we had discovered something by such addressing. Actually, we used the poster side for the picture because the envelope flap made registration of the picture too difficult. Addressing on the flap side was the result of necessity, because we didn't want to put a window in the middle of the picture.

American Heritage also was the first to successfully introduce installment payments for a magazine subscription sold by mail.

INVENTING MERGE-PURGE AND TWO-WEEK FOLLOW-UP

Eventually we were selling six products a year: *American Heritage, Horizon,* an *American Heritage* book, a *Horizon* book, an *American Heritage* children's book series and a *Horizon* children's book series.

Because we used the same outside list universe of some seven million names for all our publications, we invented merge-purge. There were no computers yet, so we did it by labeling the order cards, putting them in alphabetical order by post office and removing the duplicates—all by hand.

In mailings of seven million this primitive merge-purge was cumbersome. But it worked. (We didn't want customers to receive a mailing for a product they had already bought. We wanted them to open the mail for each of our products and not assume from the outside envelope that they had already purchased it.)

In writing this I'm struck by the fact that in the 33 years since then, except for *Smithsonian* I have almost never been involved in mailings larger than seven million.

Another innovation at *Heritage* was the recognized follow-up mailing in which we remailed the same list 14 days later. The message "recognized" that we had previously mailed the recipient and offered another chance. To save money, we eliminated the brochure in our follow-up.

WHEN WE INITIATED THE FOLLOW-UP MAILINGS
THEY PULLED 50% OF THE ORIGINAL MAILING.
THE 50% FIGURE CONTINUES TO HOLD UP TODAY
ALMOST WITHOUT FAIL WHEN WE MAIL A
CARBON-COPY FOLLOW-UP TWO WEEKS AFTER
THE ORIGINAL, RECOGNIZING THE FIRST MAILING
WITH OVERPRINTED COPY TO THE EFFECT THAT
"IF YOU MISSED THE FIRST ONE, HERE IS A
SECOND OPPORTUNITY."

The forerunner of today's popular "soft offer" was our space ad, promoting a single copy of *Heritage* for $1 with no strings; we then converted the buyer to a subscriber.

Then came the books.

The first book published by *American Heritage* was *Great Historic Places*. We sent four mailings to the active subscriber list; an astounding 33% of our active subscribers bought the book. We dropped our first mailing in January and sent a follow-up two weeks later. The offer in those mailings was built on a preprint order price (about $1 less than prepublication), which we described as the lowest price offered; we didn't say exactly how much cheaper.

We sent the third mailing in July-August, and the fourth was a follow-up two weeks later. The offer was prepublication. For subscribers to our publications, the price was always a little less than parallel offers to outsiders.

This price break to subscribers exemplifies Jim Parton's understanding of how to make the second sale.

A PIVOTAL YEAR

In 1960, we had some 365,000 subscribers to *Heritage* and about 150,000 subscribers to *Horizon*. *Horizon* up to then had never made a profit (and I don't think it ever did). My own belief is that it was too difficult to read. One of the lessons I learned from Jim Parton is that something sold by mail needs to offer some fun and enjoyment.

That same year Bruce Catton authored a book for us on the Civil War. We sold an astounding 285,000 copies by mail at $20 per copy, as well as another 75,000 copies through bookstores. To put this in context: Doubleday's big Christmas book that year was a book on Frederic Remington, the artist who painted scenes of the American West. I was told this book had a total print order of only 28,000.

Nineteen-sixty was the same year Time-Life recruited Jerry Hardy from Doubleday to start the book division. I negotiated a joint venture with Jerry to sell our Civil War book to the Time-Life subscriber list. This was the first product of Time-Life's new book division, and the mailing was quite profitable for both of us.

BENSON, ODD MAN OUT

Jim Parton used to delight in letting me know I didn't quite measure up to all the other people at *Heritage*, who were so very smart and able. As an illustration: We used to have regular management luncheons at the Harvard Club. Whenever a new issue of the magazine came out, each person would be asked to express an opinion. On several occasions I admitted, "I haven't yet read the issue and I don't feel it's all that important because I'm really selling furniture."

This response wasn't looked upon kindly by my masters at *Heritage*. But my position was upheld, as this episode shows:

Our promotion director, Frank Johnson, was at a party in Chappaqua, N.Y. Arthur Murray, the dance teacher, asked what he did. He answered, "I'm with *American Heritage*." Arthur said, "Oh yes, Katherine [Murray] subscribes to that, and you know, she just loves to take it out of the carton and put it on the bookshelf."

At *American Heritage*, we were direct-mail pioneers. I really think we were doing the best promotion mailings in the country. Much of that success stemmed from the attention we paid to mailing lists. I spent a third of my time researching lists and trying to get lists not generally on the market. I know of no mail-order company or magazine today that devotes enough effort to mailing lists.

I remember making a speech to the Direct Marketing Club in New York, then known as the Hundred Million Club. I talked about renting one list of one million people and paying $50 per thousand for one-time use of the names. Not a soul in the audience believed me because no one could conceive of paying that much when the standard price for lists was $15 per thousand. In retrospect, I believe our biggest mistake at *American Heritage* was our lack of aggressive price testing for the magazine.

HOWEVER, THE MOST IMPORTANT FACTOR FOR OUR SUCCESS WAS THE EXCELLENCE OF OUR EDITORIAL PRODUCTS.

4
RICHARD V. BENSON
AND
ASSOCIATES

Ⓘn the year 1960, *American Heritage* made its first $1 million-plus profit, an increase of 50% over the previous year. In April of the following year, I passed a dangerous milestone: I was 40 years old and was going through my own version of the normal midlife career crisis. Second in command only to Jim Parton, I was the number-one person on the business and circulation side of *American Heritage*.

It was unlikely I'd ever succeed Parton. For one thing I was incapable of managing the editorial side. Anyway, Jim was only four or five years older than I, and I wasn't going to wait 15 or 20 years until he retired.

I had other problems. I was having conflicts with Jerry Rosen, a classmate of Jim's who had joined the company. And Jim and I were having a major disagreement about my compensation.

We had established a bonus plan in 1959. As I remember, 12 of us participated in this plan. There had been discussions, when the plan was set up, about how the bonuses would be distributed. The total bonus pot was a percentage of the profits. The final resolution was that 30% of the pot was to be distributed on merit and 70% distributed proportionate to salary.

At the time, I had lobbied to reverse the percentages. For the year 1959, Dick Ketchum, one of our editors, and I received most (if not all) of the merit portion of the bonus.

The bonus pot in 1960 was substantially larger in total because of our increased profits. But despite the fact that I was sales director and sales had gone from $8 million in 1959 to $12 million in 1960, I didn't share in the merit portion of the bonus. This meant I was the only executive who had a smaller bonus for 1960 than for 1959.

As a result, after long soul searching I left the company. On September 1, 1961, I established Richard V. Benson and Associates as a direct-mail consulting company.

My original idea for my new company was to have four clients, with each of whom I'd spend one day a week. I arbitrarily allocated the fifth day to developing a proprietary business.

The idea of having four clients and spending one day a week with each of them turned out to be a poor notion. Neither the client nor I could stand each other for one full day a week. It became obvious that we had to allow more time between consultation visits for things to happen and for the client to be ready for the next step, whatever it might be.

MY SAD EXPERIENCE SELLING CAMERAS BY MAIL

My first proprietary attempt was selling home movie cameras by mail.

The first really successful syndicated product had just come into being. Al Sloan of Chicago put together a promotion for a home movie camera outfit with all the equipment anyone needed to photograph and show home movies. The outfit included camera, projector, film, lights, screen and batteries. The secret of its success was that for the first time an individual could buy a complete outfit at a one-piece price.

What Al Sloan added to the mix was the ability to assemble all the components in a one-price package. Various direct-mail marketers sold his camera outfits on installment payments. Encyclopedia companies and some other mail-order companies did very well selling this package through the mail.

Al Sloan didn't sell direct; he was a syndicator. But wasn't I smart enough to sell cameras direct? No, I wasn't.

I had no trouble convincing new parents to buy the movie outfits, but I ignored one big problem: the potential bad credit of customers whose names came from cold-compiled lists.

Even with credit reports and screening the buyers, bad debt was a horror. I hadn't taken into account the importance of a house list of creditworthy customers.

I survived a disaster, but it was a very expensive lesson.

BENSON THE CONSULTANT

My first consulting client was Time-Life Books. Columbia Record Club, the *Reporter* magazine and the advertising agency Ogilvy & Mather followed surprisingly fast.

In order to avoid the stress a common contract-expiration date might put me under, my contracts with clients were open-end, without specific expiration dates but with 90 days' notice (on either side) for termination. The only exception was Ogilvy, which was a calendar-year contract.

I really believe my use of open-end contracts was a powerful contributor to the longevity of my client relationships. My clients have stayed with me an average of more than five years. That includes some that lasted no more than three months. There is a parallel in mail.

YOU CAN EXPECT THE SAME RESULT WHEN YOU SELL "OPEN END" BY MAIL, ON A CREDIT CARD. THE CUSTOMER NEVER FACES A DIRECT RENEWAL DECISION. THE LONGEVITY OF THE CUSTOMER IS DRAMATICALLY INCREASED.

TIME-LIFE BOOKS

During the five years I worked with Time-Life Books, the division was fabulously successful. Even with my famous arrogance, I can't claim that the success was the result of anything I did; the excellence of the product was fantastic. The publisher, Jerry Hardy, declared early on, even before there was a product, "Our policy will be to give the customer more than he has any right to expect."

This was an attitude I felt we shared and developed at *American Heritage,* but no one at *Heritage* had ever summed it up in the same way. I think it is an absolutely wonderful statement of purpose. But far more important: Time-Life carried through and delivered.

An illustration of this policy is the second product of Time-Life Books, the *World Library,* a series of books each about a different country. They were 128-page books, hard-covered and full of four-color illustrations. They sold for $2.95 each.

Time-Life, in customer acquisition mailings, had no "front end" incentive offer and didn't make use of a "load up,"* so common in continuity book series.

Customers of the *World Library* continued to buy books for so long that the publisher kept increasing the total number of books in the series. I don't even remember how many books *World Library* ultimately issued, but I do remember the one book was about three South Pacific Islands.

In the five years I worked with Time-Life Books, the company did very little testing of its promotion mailings. The "control" was a package with a bed-sheet (25" × 34") brochure that succeeded so well they just never saw any need to change packages. The same format was used in each succeeding series Time-Life published throughout the years I was their consultant.

I thought they should test much more and urged them to

---

* A "load up" in a continuity book series is sending—after the first, second or third shipment—all the remaining books to the customer at one time. The customer continues to pay for the books in installments.

test new packages, but you can imagine how difficult it was to argue with the enormous success the Book Division was enjoying.

SOME STIMULATING EXPERIENCES

For many years I worked with the Columbia Record Club. As I recall, the club was the concept of Lester Wunderman, the wizard advertising man. Although the club tested many, many member acquisition approaches, nothing worked as well as their control for many years, a stamp sheet with postage-size stamps representing 100 or more records.

The prospective member chose from 6 to 12 records as his initial free premium.

There was no Ogilvy Direct when I began consulting with the agency then known as Ogilvy, Benson (no relation) & Mather in 1962. For several years the preponderance of my work with this agency was on the Shell Oil account.

Those were the days when all the major oil companies were handing out credit cards by the tens of thousands, with no customer application or credit check. Selling gasoline was an extremely competitive business. Unlike the practice at the other oil companies, Shell prechecked the mailing lists at the credit bureaus, so Shell never faced the bad-pay disasters other companies suffered.

Credit screening of lists cost Shell about $1 per name mailed, but in the long run precredit checking turned out to be cheap. In fact, the bad-pay disasters among credit card customers were so extreme that laws were passed preventing issuers from mailing credit cards without a prior application from the user.

BENSON'S RULES FOR PREMIUM SELECTION

An innovation with which I was deeply involved was a real winner. As I remember, research showed that six out of ten people who had one oil-company credit card had two or more cards. Consequently, sending out a new card was no guarantee that the customer would use his card. To promote gasoline purchase and card use, Shell gave the customer a set of steak knives after the first purchase of gasoline using the credit card.

Steak knives may seem a strange premium for buying gasoline but testing had shown the knives to be stronger than sunglasses, drinking glasses and even free gasoline. Shell gave away millions of steak knives, and later the stations sold hundreds of thousands of individual knives at 15 cents each.

The rule I developed out of this premium testing is one that has proved true time and time again:

DESIRABILITY IS THE KEY ELEMENT OF A PREMIUM. THE RELATIONSHIP OF THE PREMIUM TO THE PRODUCT ISN'T IMPORTANT.

During the past ten years calculators and watches have been my benchmark in searching for premiums for my clients. I've tried far more expensive premiums, but calculators and watches have been consistent winners.

Watches were used as premiums as early as 1960, when Fingerhut, the great direct-mail sales company, successfully used so many watches as premiums that Manny Fingerhut was for a while the largest importer of pin-lever watches in America.

A successful mail promotion I developed at Shell to reactivate dormant accounts was a $2 credit good for 60 days on the customer's credit card account.

I had used this device for a chain of discount stores. It's a great premium: It's really hard not to go to the station and buy gas when you see a $2 credit balance on your current bill from Shell. Once you again start charging gas to your account the likelihood of your continuing to buy gas on your credit card is very high.

For some time I fruitlessly wrote proposals to Ogilvy that Shell could build customer loyalty by offering individual merchandise items at discount and with extended installment payments on the credit card. I felt my reasoning was sound: A customer getting a monthly bill is more likely to continue to buy Shell gasoline than a customer with a zero balance or no bills.

We didn't invent that; retail stores had for years offered installment payments to their customers and then placed their credit cashiers in the back of the store. The customer, coming in to make a payment, had to walk by all the merchandise.

In 1963, Mobil was the first oil company to offer merchandise—an electric coffee pot. Aha! Suddenly everyone wanted to get into the merchandise business. I sourced and bought all the original products Shell sold. One of the first items was a Ram circular saw which we sold for $19.98, in six installments of $3.33.

Ogilvy & Mather and/or Shell insisted on testing a Stanley saw against the Ram saw. Stanley was a known brand name but had to be priced at $24.95.

The agency people didn't recognize the tremendous importance of major price points. At $19.98 customers would buy a saw without knowing exactly when they might use it. At $24.95 they were more likely to intend to use it immediately—or they wouldn't order. The $19.98 Ram saw was the winner by a wide margin, just as I had expected, because of the $19.98 price point. Our first mailing for Shell sold 250,000 Ram circular saws!

Later on, a multiband radio at $89.95 was the outstanding product, and Shell sold some 500,000 units a year.

We sold a wide variety of products through solo mailing packages as well as through inserts accompanying the oil company's monthly bills.

Other major oil companies followed in the merchandise business, but Shell was unique. Shell bought merchandise for its own inventory and priced it so that the customer got a special deal. Shell didn't try to maximize profits on the sale of merchandise but rather sought to build customer loyalty. Many of the major oil companies dealt with promoters (syndicators), middlemen who took the promotional risk and paid the oil company a commission for the use of its name, its lists and its collection facilities. Yes, some of these partnership promotions made money, but you can understand that with a middleman (promoter), who had to pay a 15% or 20% commission to the oil company and make a profit for himself, there was no margin left to give the customer a price break.

Two or three years into the program, Shell's accounting department raised what seemed to be a logical issue: The cost of money on all of these installment sales which weren't producing direct profit for Shell.

We set up a test plan selling a $19.98 blender in six panels, ranging from a single payment to six payments. Our first discovery may seem complicated, but it isn't if you follow the logic: The cost of money was insignificant compared to the reduction in the cost of selling we could accomplish by increasing the number of payments. Sales increased in direct proportion to the reduction in the size of the monthly payments and the increase in the number of payments.

The trend did go in steps and indicated that payments ending in .01 – .49 were not as effective as payments ending in .50–.99.

IN ALL MY EXPERIENCE SINCE THEN, I'VE FOUND IT PROFITABLE EITHER TO DECREASE THE TOTAL PRICE, BRINGING PAYMENTS DOWN TO END IN .95, OR TO TAKE IN EXTRA MONEY WITHOUT ADVERSELY AFFECTING RESPONSE BY INCREASING PAYMENTS SO THEY END IN .50–.99.

REDUCING RISK AND INCREASING RESPONSE—AT THE SAME TIME

One of Ogilvy's clients was American Express, a big-volume mailer marketing the American Express card. Like many large mailers then and now they mailed in big numbers semiannually.

I advised American Express to replace its semiannual mailings with monthly mailings to "hotline" names (people who had bought by mail within the past 30 days). I wasn't surprised by the result: improved results and reduced risk.

The reduced risk stemmed from eliminating the chance

of a mass semiannual mailing's being damaged by a major news item—Sputnik, the Cuban missile crisis, an American flag-carrier being sunk in the Gulf, a major one-day or one-week drop in the stock market, the President being killed or dying in office. The improved results came from the recency of purchase by 30-day names.

To my knowledge American Express was the first big-volume mailer in those days who wholly converted to "hotline" names and monthly mailings. Based on this ongoing experience, here's another rule I use:

THE USE OF 30-DAY NAMES WILL OVERCOME SEASONALITY AND SOMETIMES SHOW RESULTS EVEN BETTER THAN THE SEASONAL MONTH NORMS.

Three examples come to mind:
1. At an oil company, the results for the sale of an additional product were twice as good when mailed 30 days after a credit card was issued to a new customer, compared to 60 days.
2. At a publishing company, results from a book offer mailed 30 days after an individual's payment for a magazine subscription were substantially higher than when mailed 60 days after payment, or when mailed in the regular semiannual promotion mailings.
3. *Contest News-Letter,* which I published for many years, successfully mailed to the "no" responses to the sweepstakes promotions of other companies every month. If a list missed our merge-purge cutoff for the month it almost always was unprofitable when we waited until the next month to mail.

In my experience most mailers other than catalogs don't pay enough attention to recency. Very few mailers take advantage of 30-day hotline names. Very few mail even part of their annual promotion volume on a monthly basis.

Another example of the importance of premiums at Ogilvy was mail we did for Nationwide Insurance. Choosing a premium is hard work, and doing it properly requires extensive testing. For Nationwide Insurance our best premium, to enable a salesman to get an appointment with a prospect, was a Sears Craftsman hammer. Think about that and you'll realize how much imagination and work went into arriving at a hammer for a premium.

Clearly what counts is the superiority of desirability over compatibility in choosing a premium.

SEARS AND OTHER OGILVY EXPERIENCES

Another client of Ogilvy's for whom we had a big marketing breakthrough was Sears. The Hartford Sears store was five years old and had tried everything to open credit accounts, a standard Sears policy. This included the use of mass telephoning by A. J. Wood, the giant telephone marketer. After five years Sears concluded that the number of the store's accounts had reached maturity in relation to the size of the trading market.

Our assignment was to develop a program that would materially increase the number of credit accounts. We promised potential customers a free catalog and free bath towels for opening an account. Our tests proved the total number of accounts could be doubled and the total cost of this promotion would be recouped in eight months through incremental sales. A phenomenal success.

Of all the advertising agencies with which I've worked or to which I've been exposed, I was most impressed by the attention paid to and money spent for research by Ogilvy to see if the agency's advertising moved the merchandise. In those days Ogilvy employed the services of A. D. Little, one of the premier research firms, to calculate the end result of their advertising, just as you and I now do every day in direct marketing. David Ogilvy was never confused about the real purpose of advertising.

In 1967 Ogilvy had the Mercedes-Benz account. At that time Mercedes-Benz was selling about 8,000 cars a year in the United States. The first direct-mail assignment came when Mercedes found itself overstocked with diesel cars. You have to remember, at the time hardly any consumer was familiar with a diesel car.

Ogilvy came up with what I believe was the first automobile manufacturer's rebate. The offer was for the prospect to go to a dealer and make a deal for a new car; Mercedes North American would then pay for the first year's fuel.

Based on an average car traveling 12,000 miles a year and the current price of diesel fuel, this offer averaged $120. Hank Bernhard, one of the best marketers I've ever been associated with, was the senior account executive. Ed McLean, well known in direct marketing circles, was the copywriter on the account. The mailing package was one of the first six-page letters mailed in mass: It was sent to 500,000 people. The mailing attracted enough buyers to the dealerships to sell $3,500,000 worth of cars.

In his speech upon accepting the Direct Marketing Association's Gold Mailbox award for the Mercedes-Benz mailing, David Ogilvy was kind enough to say, "We have also had the extreme good fortune of having access to the counseling of Dick Benson."

SOME FLOPS TO BALANCE OUT THE WINNERS

I would certainly be remiss if I didn't mention two failures (my wording). One was Ogilvy's and one was mine with Ogilvy's money.

1. When the *Economist* magazine decided to make a major expansion in the United States, the assignment went to Ogilvy. If memory serves, the first mailing consisted of 18 separate test-panels—testing formats, size of mailing package, offers and lists.

   As was only too common at Ogilvy, just one creative package was used. This means the same copy was used for a double-addressed closed-face envelope package (with its implicit space limitations) as for a 9"×12" format and for all the other formats and sizes as well. I believe this was a failure because of the test design and because the expense brought us too little information. The *Economist* did launch successfully.

The Ogilvy argument is that statistically you can change only one ingredient at a time. Yes, statistically that's irrefutable; but it's very poor direct mail. There's never enough test money available to test every ingredient, and the idea of testing the same package (copy) in a monarch size and a 9"×12" size is, in my opinion, ludicrous.

The chances of getting a winning mailing are vastly improved by testing total creative packages, with the lists and the offer constant, but with each package consistent to the size and format necessary to doing the best job. The goal is success, not statistical purity in original testing.

Who cares whether size or color or graphics or words is most important? What's needed is an economic success.

Here's another opinion: After the offer the letter is the most important ingredient in a package. I've seen many successful letter-only packages but never a winning brochure-only package. As a result, I believe testing letters is paramount.

2. In the fall of 1970 I conceived a newsletter about tax shelters. Ed Bursk, then Dean of the Harvard Business School, supplied the editorial content. The letter was meant to be fun and to provide the reader with conversation about leasing airplanes for profit, or raising cows, or second homes for rental (i.e., to be the first on the block to have inside information and know about these exotic investments).

The test mailing was successful and in January, 1971, we went ahead with the launch mailing. At this point the bottom fell out of the stock market. The Dow Jones industrial average registered 512 and no one was interested in a newsletter about tax shelters when people were losing their shirts in the market.

Ogilvy & Mather had financially backed me in this venture and we ended up losing $300,000.

I must say Ogilvy never gave me a hard time about the loss. I remained their consultant for many more years, a total of 17 in all.

5
COOKBOOKS,
THE IRS
AND
OTHER NOBLE
EXPERIMENTS

THE CULINARY SOCIETY—MY POSITIVE-OPTION EXPERIMENT

The Culinary Society was a cookbook club. It was another of my proprietary ventures at Benson Associates.

The idea was tested and sound: Both Book-of-the Month Club and the Doubleday Book Club had, and still have, cookbook clubs. In those days each of them had a membership level of roughly 125,000.

I had a better idea (so I thought). I decided to reinvent the wheel. My experience with the various Thing-of-the-Month Clubs—and with "negative option" sales in general—indicated that millions of people disliked this method of selling.

"Negative option" means that the publisher will ship each month unless the member specifically declines within a set period of time.) It seemed clear to me that there was a great opportunity to have a "positive" option club. My idea: The customer had to return the announcement card to *get* the current selection rather than returning the order form to *reject* the selection.

Our membership acquisition package incorporated an "Everybody Wins Sweepstakes" which had as its bottom prize a kitchen computer. The computer was actually a wheel on a card, a slide rule for converting weights and measures.

Membership acquisition was super-successful and the Culinary Society reached a membership level of 125,000. A great success? No! The members didn't buy any books. It was a disaster.

There was a good reason why there weren't then—and still, as far as I know, aren't now,—any positive option Thing-of-the-Month Clubs. Doubleday and the other club operators knew what they were doing. I didn't. Mine wasn't a better idea. The success of Thing-of-the-Month clubs depends a great deal on the Inertia Factor: The member doesn't bother to send in the card refusing the current selection.

Moral: The next time you think you have a revolutionary idea, be sure to do a better job than I did of checking *why* other people aren't doing it.

(Note: I was following a very good basic rule for entering the mail-order business. Look for winners and see if you can add some twist or bring some extra talent to do it better. In this case, our extra benefit was too different... a bad idea.)

I'm not alone in trying to reinvent the wheel and being wrong. Consider the catalogs that have failed because they thought they could beat the inventory problem by having all merchandise drop-shipped from the manufacturer. Shipping becomes a nightmare when you have to depend on a large number of sources.

Others have tried to cause excitement by having all new items in every catalog. This leads to inventory problems for two reasons: (1) Some items will be losers; (2) The catalog doesn't have the ability to repeat moneymaking winners.

I strongly suggest, if you have what you think is a unique and totally different idea, that you not underrate the competition. Many, many smart operators have been there before you. Don't under any circumstances sell the competition short.

THE *NEW REPUBLIC:* WE'RE *TOO* SUCCESSFUL

The *New Republic,* the liberal weekly magazine published in Washington, D.C., became our client. At the time the magazine had a total circulation of 38,000. The magazine was 50 years old and was a perennial money loser. The publisher, Gilbert Harrison, cared about what he was doing, and he could afford the losses. I admired him because personally and editorially he was willing to stand up and speak out for what he believed.

We developed a charter offer to celebrate the beginning of the *New Republic's* second 50 years. Our offer was a subscription for three months priced at only $2. The $2 price was set because we wanted to go for cash and $2 was the largest amount of money that the public would send in cash. At this price there was no check or money order decision. Even today, $2 is the most cash people will mail.

In order to convert (second sale) the three-month introductory subscriptions, we had to start mailing renewal efforts immediately at the beginning of the original subscription. Our inducement to the subscriber was to reduce the price of the renewal by $2—in effect giving the customer back his original payment or making the original three-month subscription free.

At the end of 13 of months promoting this offer and the subsequent conversion renewal offer, we had increased circulation by 190% and had recovered all initial promotion costs, conversion costs and the incremental cost of copies served.

Our services were terminated because of our success. At this point Gil Harrison felt he could bring in a major executive to help him publish the magazine. One of the responsibilities of the new man would be circulation promotion.

At the time we left the *New Republic's* circulation had risen to 110,000. Not much later, the *New Republic* reached a peak circulation of 138,000, but for the next 20 years and even to this day, the circulation has been level at roughly 100,000.

OLD AMERICAN INSURANCE

The president of Old American was Mr. Joe McGee. I regularly referred to McGee, Martin Baier, his marketing director, and Max Ross, the creative director, as my "gentlemanly gentlemen" clients.

Together they managed a very successful mail-order insurance company, an outstanding example of understanding the importance of the second sale. The basic product they promoted for an initial sale, to build their "mother list," was a low face-value life insurance policy marketed to older people. In earlier days, this type of policy was known as burial insurance.

Elsewhere in these pages I discuss the importance of establishing a "bogey" (the highest acceptable cost of acquisition of a customer) by calculating the lifetime value of a customer. Long before I worked with Old American, they were using a bogey based on a 10-year value of their initial policy. More than anyone else with whom I've worked, Old American understood the concept of using a low-cost product to build a mother list of customers to whom they could sell additional products.

Old American had some 11 or 12 additional products. The company promoted one of those products each month to the mother list of life insurance policyholders. The company profits stemmed from these additional sales.

A comparison and contrast: The major insurance companies I later consulted with not only didn't try to sell additional policies; they didn't even know which customers bought multiple policies from them. Trying to cross-sell a different policy to a policyholder was a foreign concept.

Even with the problem of protecting agent commissions, I'm constantly astounded by what a poor job the insurance companies do in capitalizing on their great asset: policyholders. Agent protection aside, every company has a tremendous proportion of so-called orphan policies (policies placed by agents who no longer represent the company).

A simple illustration: As we all know, surveys show that the public doesn't want to talk to insurance agents. We also know that a physical examination is another major hurdle to buying life insurance and provides an excuse for procrastination.

But did you know that many companies will issue a second, different policy, equal to the original policy, for up to a year or even longer, without a physical examination? Did any company ever offer you such an opportunity? Some companies will never understand how to milk their customer lists.

One of Old American's most innovative promotions was an endorsement package mailed over the letterhead of a funeral home and in a black-bordered envelope. You *know* that's an envelope the recipient will open.

A project we conceived for Old American was a club for older people. The club was built around a newsletter, "The Informed American." This was a straight adaptation of our idea to create a low-cost product that could stand on its own but would build a "captive" prospect list for the insurance company. Either because our concept wasn't good enough or because we failed in our implementation, we weren't able to build the club to a self-sustaining size. We sold it to a newsletter publisher.

Our most effective work at Old American was moving the company's marketing philosophy along to implementation. The three people who were concerned with marketing had worked together for a number of years. They were all true gentlemen who would never ruffle one another's feathers. Our job, as I saw it, was to force decisions on matters that had been put off because unanimity was lacking among the three. (A consultant can and should do this. The consultant becomes the bad guy, but the internal relationships aren't upset.)

Martin Baier was a pioneer in list segmentation. His first work was regression analysis using census demographics and SCFs (sectional center facilities). He published an article in the *Harvard Business Review* describing his research in this area. As I understand it, his article was the first impetus persuading the Bureau of the Census to break down its demographic information by zip codes. This change was the foundation of our modern day "tree" analysis for segmenting lists by zip code. Martin tells me he has gone well beyond the "tree", but I must confess I just don't understand what it is that he does now.

THE INTERNAL REVENUE SERVICE

The Internal Revenue Service is certainly a strange account for a small direct-mail agency!

I don't recall how we first got involved, but I'm sure it was by way of referral, since it certainly wasn't an account we'd have chased.

Our assignment was to rewrite some 300 form letters. The letters the IRS was using were stilted and sounded as if they had been written 50 years earlier. (They probably had been.) We were to make them more one-on-one, sounding as if a real person had written them.

We did our best to make the letters more friendly. It's bad enough to get a letter from the IRS, but it helps a little if the message—however revolting—seems a little more personal.

The major reason for our accepting a contract with the IRS was a discussion with their representatives: If we did this job successfully, they'd (so help me!) give us a crack at simplifying the 1040 form along with the impenetrable instructions for filling it out.

You can't imagine the frustrations of discussing 300 individual letters with several government bureaucrats. Most of the discussions regarded the cosmic question of whether a particular word was just exactly the right word. Everybody thinks he's a copywriter. (Except me. I am not and I don't try to be.)

Think of the amount of second-guessing that would come up if you had the assignment, subject to government intervention, of rewriting the income tax instructions as well as the 1040 form. I'm positive it's just as well we never were given that assignment.

The biggest truth I learned from this job was that government contracts weren't for us. Not only did we have to negotiate a fee before we started, but we also had to substantiate the fee with endless evidence of the completed work and a record of hours spent by different people involved at varying hourly rates.

A small shop isn't used to keeping time sheets. How do you put a time clock on freelance copywriters? Do you count the time you think about the copy when you aren't actually pounding the keyboard?

There were unrealistic limits on the hourly rates for different skills. As I recall, the highest hourly rate for even the principals was $12.50, or $100 a day. Using a strict interpretation of the rules, we couldn't and didn't make a profit. I'm sure you can make a profit with a government contract, but you almost need a specialist who understands the rules and the exceptions. For us to make a profit, as we saw it, would have meant fudging the hours spent on the project. We lost money!

BRECK'S

Breck's was a nifty-gifty catalog out of Boston. It emphasized merchandise with $1 price points. After I'd made several attempts to convince Tom Foster of Foster & Gallagher (another catalog) to try a sweepstakes, we sold the concept to Luther Breck. He became one of the first cataloguers, if not the very first, to use sweepstakes. We subsequently developed several sweepstakes promotions for him.

One sweepstakes we created for Breck's had an unusual twist. It had a bottom prize for 1,000 people, who could choose anything from the catalog. If you entered this sweepstakes, you had to go through the catalog to find out what you might like to win and tell us on the entry form which item you wanted if you became one of the winners.

A bigger success for Breck's than sweepstakes was a free premium with any order. I've used this device with several catalogs. I believe giving the same premium to every buyer is psychologically stronger than giving different premiums based on the size of the order or demanding an order of a minimum dollar size.

This concept of a gift with every order seems to terrify clients who are afraid their customers will rip them off by buying the cheapest item in the catalog in order to get the premium. (Actually, rip-off is a minimal problem. Very few customers take advantage of this loophole. Taking this small risk has been far more successful than requiring a specific minimum dollar purchase to qualify for the premium.)

Our best premium at Breck's was a mystery or surprise gift. The beauty of the mystery gift is that it allows you to use bits and pieces of leftover inventory.

We tested mailing the Breck's catalog in an envelope with a separate letter and an extra order card. It was a success economically but Breck's printer couldn't handle the volume, and the concept died because of logistics. I've used this format of mailing a catalog in an envelope a number of times since then with small catalogs—usually successfully.

The advantage of mailing a catalog in an envelope is that you can have a separate letter—which attracts much more attention than the letters or messages that often appear on the inside cover of a catalog. You also can enclose an extra order form, giving you a better chance to get a second order at a later date, when the customer can then use the order form bound in the catalog.

Breck's had a promotion for amaryllis bulbs, for which we prepared the mailing package. Our art director, Dick Browner, came up with a spectacular concept in which, with each additional unfolding of the brochure, the plant seemed to grow larger. The mailing won a major award for design. To our chagrin the package wasn't profitable. That says something about the relationship between art awards and profitability.

With the advent of inflation and the fact that most $1.00 goods just won't sell at $1.10, we faced a continuing reduction in the amount of available goods we could include in the catalog. Finally we reached the point at which we couldn't deliver perceived value at a $1.00 price point. Picking and packing fulfillment costs also kept rising. The catalog was no longer profitable.

For several years we had urged Luther Breck to test a new catalog with items at higher price points to take advantage of his lists and his ability to start a new catalog as an incremental business. But no test of this concept was ever made.

It's sad how many businesses refuse to face up to the life cycles of business and spend money on research and development of new product lines. This same refusal, unfortunately, takes place at many companies that have plateaued, yet are still profitable.

My impression is that hard-goods and packaged-goods manufacturers are much more aware of product life cycles and the need for new product lines than are people who do business by mail.

The Breck's catalog was finally closed down and became a casualty of the relentless pressure of increasing inflation.

Dick Leventer was marketing director of Breck's. He had resigned to join another catalog, but after looking at the location he and his family decided to stay in Boston. The scuttlebutt at Breck's was that because he had resigned and come back, Breck's now owned him and he had no future. I was impressed with Dick's abilities and felt he would leave again at the first opportunity, so I hired him to work at our agency.

When I did this, Luther Breck immediately fired us. From my standpoint, it was a good trade.

6
THE
ADMIRAL BYRD
SOCIETY

I n 1965 Ernest Frawley, an old friend who was business manager of the *Harvard Business Review*, called me about an idea the Dean of the Business School had.

The Dean's idea, to raise funds, was to form the Admiral Byrd Society—selling a trip around the world, including both the North and South Poles and all the continents.

This would be the first public trip circling the world north to south rather than east to west. The trip would be limited to 60 people and priced at $10,000 per person. One big problem was the available promotion budget: only $5,000.

I accepted the challenge even though it was obvious we couldn't possibly make a profit.

My cynical hindsight tells me the Admiral Byrd Society was born when Ed Bursk and a friend of his who had been with Byrd on one of his polar expeditions were sitting around over drinks, brainstorming for a project for the friend, who needed a job.

The famous freelance copywriter Hank Burnett was our creative chief at the time. Hank did a wonderful personalized seven-page letter, which we reproduced by automatic typewriter. (I think it was the first mass-mailed letter of that length.)

The second paragraph of Hank's brilliant letter said, "It will cost you $10,000 and about 26 days of your time. Frankly, you will endure some discomfort and may even face some danger."

One of our major problems was the choice of which lists to mail. We ended up mailing to members of the Young Presidents Club, owners of two-engine private airplanes, Arabian horse breeders and owners of boats of 40 feet or longer.

The promotion package had no response device because I frankly didn't know what to use. An order card seemed totally inadequate.

The trip was sold out, and by reconfiguring the plane 72 people were able to go. The total promotion costs stayed within the $5,000 budget. In addition, we actually had a small waiting list of people who had signed up to go. The Direct Marketing Association gave us their Gold Mailbox Award for this promotion. I think this mailing was a near-perfect example of proper list research.

The Admiral Byrd Society mailing was such a breakthrough that I'm reproducing the letter in its entirety:

Edward C. Bursk
Soldiers Field
Boston, Massachusetts
02163

Please reply to me in care of:
Editor
Harvard Business Review
Transpolar Expedition
Admiral Richard E. Byrd Polar Center
18 Tremont Street
Boston, Massachusetts 02108

As Chairman of the Admiral Richard E. Byrd Polar Center, it is my privilege to invite you to become a member of an expedition which is destined to make both news and history.

It will cost you $10,000 and about 26 days of your time. Frankly, you will endure some discomfort, and may even face some danger.

On the other hand, you will have the rare privilege of taking part in a mission of great significance for the United States and the entire world. A mission, incidentally, which has never before been attempted by man.

You will personally have the chance to help enrich mankind's fund of knowledge about two of the last earthly frontiers, the polar regions.

I am inviting you to join a distinguished group of 50 people who will fly around the world longitudinally, over both poles, on an expedition which will commemorate Admiral Richard E. Byrd's first Antarctic Flight in 1929.

Among the highlights of this transpolar flight—the first commercial flight ever to cross both poles and touch down on all continents —will be stopovers at the American military/scientific bases at Thule, Greenland, and McMurdo Sound, Antarctica.

Because this expedition has the interest and support of much of the Free World, you and your fellow members will be honored guests (in many cases, even celebrities) at state and diplomatic receptions throughout the itinerary. You will have the opportunity to meet and talk with some of the world's important national leaders and public figures, such as Pope Paul VI, the Emperor of Japan, General Carlos Romulo and many others who are already a part of history.

By agreeing to join this expedition, you will, in a sense, establish yourself in history too. For you will become a Founding Trustee of the new Admiral Richard E. Byrd Polar Center, sponsor of the expedition.

Your biography will be recorded in the Center's archives, available to future historians. The log, photographs and memorabilia of the expedition will be permanently displayed in the Center. And your name will be inscribed, with those of the other expedition members, on a bronze memorial tablet.

Before I continue with the details of the expedition, let

me tell you more about the Byrd Polar Center and the reasoning which led to its establishment this summer.

Located in Boston, home of the late Admiral and point of origin for each of his seven expeditions, this nonprofit institution will house, catalog and preserve the papers and records of both Admiral Byrd and other Arctic and Antarctic explorers.

But the Center will have a more dynamic function than merely to enshrine the past. It will be a vital, viable organization devoted to furthering peaceful development of the polar regions, particularly Antarctica.

It will become, in effect, this country's headquarters for investigation and research into the scientific and commercial development of the poles. The Center will sponsor, support, initiate and conduct studies and expeditions. It will furnish comprehensive data or technical assistance to the United States, or to any university, institution, foundation, business organization or private individual legitimately interested in polar development.

In other words, the Center has set for itself a course which the Admiral before his death endorsed wholeheartedly. He foresaw that mankind would one day benefit enormously from development of Antarctica's vast potential. And he perceived that Antarctica's unique and diverse advantages and resources might be best developed by private capital in a free-enterprise context.

The Byrd Polar Center is dedicated to these objectives. And the essential purpose of this commemorative expedition is to dramatize the role that private enterprise—and private citizens—can play in the opening of these last frontiers.

At the same time, the expedition should help prove a few other important points. It should demonstrate the feasibility of shrinking the world through longitudinal navigation. It should also help blaze a trail for commercial air travel over the South Pole. Presently, to fly from Chile to Australia, you must go by way of Los Angeles, even though a straight line trans-Antarctic route would be far shorter.

There is another factor I should mention, one which I

think lends a certain urgency to the work of the Center. Development of the polar regions enjoys a high official priority in the Soviet Union—higher, some believe, than in the United States.

The Center's activities can provide a tangible effective complement to those of our own government, and over the long term, contribute meaningfully to preservation of the Arctic and Antarctic regions for peaceful purposes.

These objectives, I think you will agree, are entirely valid. And important for the future of humanity. It is for this reason that the inaugural activity of the Byrd Polar Center will be an expedition of such scope and magnitude.

The expedition will be led by Commander Fred G. Dustin, veteran of six polar expeditions, advisor to Admiral Byrd and one of the intrepid group which spent the winter of 1934 in Little America on Byrd's Antarctic Expedition II. Commander Dustin is a member of the U.S. Antarctica Committee and President of the Byrd Polar Center.

Considered the ranking American authority on the polar regions, Fred Dustin is probably better qualified to lead this expedition—and brief members on virtually every aspect of the polar regions—than any man on earth. The Center and the expedition are fortunate to have Commander Dustin, as you will discover should you decide to participate.

The flight will be made in a specially outfitted, four-engine commercial jet with lounge-chair-and-table cabin configuration. A full flight crew of six will be headed by Captain Hal Neff, former pilot of Air Force One, the Presidential plane. Special clothing and equipment, such as Arctic survival gear, will be provided by the expedition and carried aboard the plane.

The expedition members will meet in Boston on the evening of November 7, 1968, for briefing and a reception and send-off party with the Governor of Massachusetts, Mayor of Boston, local officials and directors of the Byrd Polar Center. Next day, we will take off, head due north from Boston's Logan International Airport and follow this itinerary (as I have not yet visited all these places myself, I have drawn on the descriptions submitted to me by Commander Dustin and the other experienced people who have planned the expedition):

Thule, Greenland

Far above the Arctic Circle, past the chill reaches of Baffin Bay, lies desolate Thule, the northernmost U.S. air base. Almost 400 miles further north than the northern tip of Alaska, Thule was originally surveyed as a possible military site by Admiral Byrd and Commander Dustin. Here, in the deepening Arctic winter, you will get your first taste of the rigors of polar existence. You will have the chance to inspect the installations and meet the men for whom Arctic survival is a way of life.

North Pole

According to those who have crossed the North Pole, you will completely lose your day-night orientation. Sunrise and sunset can occur within minutes of each other, a strange and unforgettable phenomenon. After Thule, you will cross the geographic North Pole, just as Admiral Byrd did in his pioneering trans-Arctic flight with Floyd Bennett in 1926. A memorial flag will be dropped.

Anchorage, Alaska

After crossing the Pole, the plane will bank into a 90-degree left turn and head south, over the Arctic Ocean and Beaufort Sea, past Mt. McKinley, North America's highest peak, and on to Anchorage. There, you will meet the Governor and key officials.

Tokyo, Japan

The highlight of your stopover in Japan will be an opportunity to meet the Emperor and Premier. (Fishing; excursion to Hakone and Atami by bullet train; tea ceremony at private homes.)

Manila, Philippines

General Carlos Romulo, the legendary patriot and statesman, an old friend of Admiral Byrd, will give the

expedition a warm welcome in Manila. (Folklore performance; hunting for duck, deer, wild boar and a special species of water buffalo; fishing for tuna and marlin.)

You will note that here and elsewhere we have prear-
ranged a considerable amount of hunting, fishing and so
on. These activities are optional. (Members of the expedition will be asked to indicate their preferences 30 days
before the flight.) For those who do not want to participate in any of these events, there will be sightseeing and/
or golf.

Darwin, Australia

Hard by the Timor Sea, tropical Darwin offers some of the
world's most superb beaches. You will have time not only
to sample the sand and water sports, but to see Australia's
great outback. With its spectacular chasms, canyons and
gorges, the rarely visited outback is a scenic match for our
own West.

Sydney, Australia

You can look forward to an enthusiastic reception in Sydney by the Prime Minister and government officials. For
one thing, Australia is on particularly good terms with the
United States. For another, Australia has traditionally been
in the vanguard of nations involved in Antarctic explo-
ration and development. (Hunting for kangaroo, crocodile,
buffalo, wild boar, duck and geese; or offshore fishing for
rifle fish, salmon and giant grouper.)

Christchurch, New Zealand

This is our staging point for the flight to Antarctica, and it
couldn't be more appropriate. Most of the early expeditions
departed from New Zealand, and Admiral Byrd is still considered a national hero there. New Zealand is Antarctic-
conscious and its people take almost a proprietary interest
in the frozen continent. You will be something of a celebrity
in New Zealand, and can expect a thoroughly enjoyable
visit while the expedition awaits favorable weather reports
from McMurdo Sound. (Deer hunting—where deer are so
plentiful that they pay a bounty; fishing for all of the great

species of marlin—in an area known for the greatest marlin fishing in the world—also mako shark.)

McMurdo Sound, Antarctica

I am told that only a total eclipse of the sun is comparable, in emotional impact, to the first sight of Antarctica. Once experienced, neither can be forgotten. If you prove to be like most who have seen Antarctica, you will need somehow, someday, to return. And when you do, the emotional impact will be just as profound. That is what the Antarctic veterans say.

For Antarctica exists well beyond the boundaries of the world you know. You will see there a sun you have never before seen, breathe air you have never before breathed. You will see menacing white mountains towering for thousands of feet over a black ocean in which, with luck, you might survive for 45 seconds. You will see the awesome Ross Ice Shelf, as large as France, with its 50- to 200-foot ice cliffs cleaving the sea for 400 miles. You will see the active volcano, Mt. Erebus, 13,000 feet of fire and ice.

And you will also see the huts, so well preserved they seem to have been inhabited only yesterday, which Shackleton used in 1908 and the ill-fated Scott in 1911. Antarctica, apparently, is not subject to the passage of time as we know it. At McMurdo Base, you will meet the military men and scientists who inhabit this strange, alien territory. And you will inhabit it for a while, too—long enough to feel its bone-chilling cold, to hear its timeless silence, to perceive, at the very edge of your composure, the terror of its mindless hostility to human beings.

While you are there, you will learn, as few men have ever had the opportunity to learn, about Antarctica. You will learn about survival, but more important, about what men must accomplish to truly open this formidable frontier.

South Pole

Admiral Byrd was the first man to fly over the South Pole. In all of history, probably fewer than 200 men have crossed the Pole, by air or otherwise. As a member of this expedition, you will join that select group.

Punta Arenas, Chile

From the South Pole, you will fly to Punta Arenas, on the tortuous Strait of Magellan, which separates continental South America from bleak Tierra del Fuego. The visit here will be brief, but you should get some idea of the flavor of this nearly forgotten outpost.

Rio de Janiero, Brazil

This memorable stopover will include a diplomatic reception. You will also have a chance to relax and sample the sights and sounds of fabulous Rio (special plane to Bela Horizonte for hunting boar, duck, jaguar, panther, water buffalo, crocodile and deer).

Dakar, Senegal

You may never have expected to see Dakar, but you will on this expedition. (Tribal dancing; safari.)

Rome, Italy

No trip would be complete without a stop in Rome, where we will be received enthusiastically. During our stay there we will have a private audience with the Pope.

London, England

From London, the expedition will fly back across the Atlantic and terminate with a debriefing, critique and farewell dinner in Boston, on December 3.

As mementos of the expedition, you will receive a leather-bound, personalized copy of the logbook and a piece of the fabric from Admiral Byrd's original plane, mounted in crystal. You will also be presented with a framed certificate from the Admiral Richard E. Byrd Polar Center, affirming your appointment as a Founding Trustee and expressing appreciation for your interest in, contributions to and efforts on behalf of the Center and its objectives. In the future, you will be kept fully advised of the plans and activities of the center, and be invited to participate to whatever extent you wish. And of course, you will have lifelong access to the Center's archives and services.

Most important, you will take back with you a once-in-a-lifetime experience. The day may come when journeys to and over the poles are commonplace. But today, the privilege is available to very few.

It is true, I think, that this privilege does carry responsibility with it. By the time you return, you will have received a comprehensive indoctrination course in the polar regions by the world's leading authorities. Your responsibility will be to make the most of the knowledge you will gain, to become an active advocate—perhaps even a disciple—of Polar research and development.

It is a responsibility which, I trust, will weigh easily upon you. For once the polar air has been absorbed into your bloodstream, there is no cure. Like others who have been stricken, you will probably find yourself reading every word you can find on the North and South Poles. And, most likely, thinking about your next trip.

But first of all, you must decide about this trip. If you have a sense of adventure, a certain pioneering spirit, and if the prospect of taking part in a mission of worldwide significance and historical importance appeals to you, perhaps you should consider joining the expedition. It is doubtful that you will ever have another chance like this.

Obviously, you can't make a decision of this magnitude instantly. But a word of caution: reservations will be accepted in the order received—a total of only 60, including ten standbys. The departure date, remember, is November 8, 1968, so there is little time to waste.

The price of $10,000 includes food and beverages, all accommodations (the best available under all circumstances), transportation, special clothing, insurance, side excursions—virtually everything except your travel to and from Boston.

Money received will go into escrow at the United States Trust Company in Boston until the time of the flight. To the extent that revenues from the trip will exceed costs, the activities of the Polar Center will be accelerated.

To reserve your place in the expedition, just drop me a note on your letterhead or personal stationery, with your deposit check for $2,500, made out to the United States Trust Company. Incidentally, if anything prevents your leaving as planned, you can send another in your place; otherwise, cancellations cannot be accepted later that 30 days before departure.

If you have further questions, please write to me in care of the Transpolar Expedition, Admiral Richard E. Byrd Polar Center, 18 Tremont Street, Boston, Massachusetts 02108.

I hope we may hear from you soon—and that we will welcome you to the expedition.

Sincerely yours,

Edward C. Bursk
ECB:ehk

P.S. We have made arrangements for a professional camera crew to accompany the flight, and as a result we will be able to provide you with a short film clip and sound tape of your experiences.

Robert H. Jones, a talented copywriter, was so taken with the success of the Byrd promotion that he became an entrepreneur and "knocked it off" (i.e., copied the approach).

Bob developed a trip that was, in effect, a boys' night out—a celebration of life. He took over an Irish castle, stocked it with serving wenches and built his trip around it. He succeeded so well that he repeated the junket annually for several years.

The best story I recall about Bob's venture is this one: Bob had assembled his group at the New York airport. As they entered the plane, the attendants directed them to coach seats. You can imagine the complaints, because these people had paid a hefty price for what Bob had represented as a glamorous trip.

Never at a loss for words, Bob squelched the complaints with the bright explanation, "Fellows, you don't understand. There are only 17 seats up there. There are just too many of us."

Nodding their understanding, his travelers dutifully took their seats.

7
ENCYCLOPEDIAS, MAGAZINES, INSURANCE AND WINE

ENCYCLOPAEDIA BRITANNICA

The Chicago company that published the *Encyclopaedia Britannica* was headed by Senator Benton of Benton & Bowles advertising fame. The encyclopedia was sold door-to-door, but the company also had a thriving mail-order business selling products—mostly books—to encyclopedia buyers.

(A note here: *Britannica* has always used the classic spelling, "Encyclopaedia;" common U.S. usage is "encyclopedia.")

The year *Britannica* retained us coincided roughly with the emergence of so-called syndicated merchandise. Syndicated merchandise here refers to big-ticket products for which a promoter or manufacturer has prepared and tested a mailing package that others could use to sell a single item in installment payments. Books had been syndicated for years prior to this time.

In an effort to expand beyond publishing, *Britannica* wanted to sell hard goods. Senator Benton wasn't sure about the propriety of *Britannica* selling merchandise, since the company was, first of all, an educational company.

An initial test was made. A typewriter was sold over the *Britannica* name, versus the same typewriter sold by an unknown company. All mail was sent to the owners of the encyclopedia.

THE NO-NAME MAILING PULLED ONLY 50% AS WELL AS THE MAILING USING THE *BRITANNICA* LETTERHEAD. THESE ARE PARTICULARLY STRONG RESULTS, BUT IN MY EXPERIENCE THERE IS ALWAYS A MEANINGFUL (AT LEAST 50%) INCREASE IN RESULTS FROM A HOUSE MAILING TO CUSTOMER LISTS.

THE WEEKLY READER

The Weekly Reader was a publishing company owned (at the time we were hired) by Wesleyan University in Middletown, Connecticut.

The company's basic business was tabloids published for use in classrooms. You may remember *Current Events* from your own school days. This was one of that group of publications.

As an extension of classroom products, they had additional product lines, which they sold directly to the home.

The *Summer Weekly Reader* is a tabloid sent to children at their homes. It's sold through mailings to teachers at their schools and includes take-home subscription forms, which the teacher is encouraged to have the student take home and return. The teacher is given a premium based on the number of returned forms.

Another of Weekly Reader's product lines was a series of hardcover books sold in the same manner, as well as by mailings sent directly to the home. The Weekly Reader Book Club was sold by subscription, $6 for six books in one year.

When Benson, Stagg and Associates was retained in 1964, the book club had a membership of 280,000 and an almost nonexistent profit—just $10,000. On our advice, the structure of the club was changed from annual subscription to automatic shipment, with each book billed individually at a price of $2. Our copy theme for acquiring new subscribers was based on the line: "Do you want your child (preschool through fourth grade) to go to college? Teach him to read."

Over a period of time, we tripled the size of the club. Our first move was to be much more aggressive with teacher premiums, within rules promulgated by Wesleyan University. (The basic rule was that the premium had to be useful in the classroom.) Our mission was to develop a desirable premium that could be used in the classroom, but at the teacher's option; and without our specifically suggesting it, the teacher might well want to take it home.

One of our most successful premiums was a Polaroid camera, even though it required some convoluted copy to make it really seem to be a classroom item.

Order slips were provided for the teacher to send home with each child, requesting that the parents say, "Yes," they wanted to subscribe or, "No," they didn't want to subscribe. Our major innovation for the teacher promotion was to count not only Yes subscription forms but those saying No in the teacher's premium quota. The teacher then had every reason to require the child to return the slip from home whether the answer was "Yes" or "No".

In just four years the size of the book club tripled, reaching a membership level of 850,000 and a profit of almost $2 million.

As so often happens, in order to make budgeted profits an extra cycle was added in each ensuing year. While this tended to increase the specific year's profits, it didn't do much for total profits. The lifetime purchase of books for each starter increased very little with 12 cycles a year versus the original six cycles.

THIS IS PROBABLY TO BE EXPECTED, AS ONE OF THE BETTER RULES OF THUMB I KNOW IS THAT CONTINUITIES AVERAGE 5 1/2-6 SHIPMENTS.

Time-Life Books was the only major exception to this rule. They experienced a much higher number of purchases. This was the result of having no "special offer" up front and of the excellence of their product. I suspect Time-Life was better off on balance, but no one will ever really know, because as far as I know they didn't test special acquisition offers.

Very recently I've seen some special first-book offers by Time-Life. We shall see if they change their promotion for continuities as time goes by.

By the way, after a lapse of a number of years, I am once again a consultant to the publishers of the *Weekly Reader.*

INSURANCE COMPANY OF NORTH AMERICA—THE INA

The INA is one of the largest insurance companies in the country. It was a great coup for our agency, to land them as an account, particularly because the assignment was so unusual.

Our brief was to devise one series of mailings to home-owner-insurance policyholders and another to auto insurance policyholders, with the goal of increasing safety and reducing claims.

We developed a series of monthly mailings, each of which included a premium. The copy was about one or another safety factor for policyholders of each type of insurance.

A typical mailing was one in which we included a packet of chemicals to place in the water at the base of the family Christmas tree to keep the needles from dropping so quickly. The copy went on to discuss checking the lights before putting them on the tree and the importance of the UL label on electric appliances.

Another mailing included nonslip treads for the bathtub and copy about the hazards one might face in the bathroom.

This series to home policyholders showed a reduction in claims paid of $7 for every $1 we spent.

For the auto policyholder, one mailing included a sweepstakes for a set of free tires and copy regarding tire safety, as well as directions for using a dime to measure for tread safety. Response to this sweepstakes with only one modest prize was phenomenal.

But the series of mailings to auto-policy customers showed absolutely no improvement in claims reduction when compared to a control group of nonrecipients. Why? Our conclusion was that auto accidents are caused by a lapse of concentration. Safety education can't overcome such lapses.

When it came time for us to roll out the campaign to all of the company's homeowner policyholders, our leader at the INA had a physical breakdown and was out of action indefinitely. The insurance company had experienced a bad year due to catastrophes. No budget was available. If our leader had been there, we might have received money for the rollout of our successful promotion; but the reality is that there are no medals in corporate life for a new person to pursue someone else's brief. No budget money was forthcoming.

Since those days insurance companies have adjusted their rates so that the customer now finds it more economical to accept a deductible on his policy, eliminating many of the small claims that had been such a problem.

This was one of the major disappointments of my career. After all, how often do any of us get the opportunity to do something *good*—something to make us feel that by reducing accidents we'd left our footprints in the sands of time?

CRESTA BLANCA

Herb Drake, a particularly fine gentleman with Guild Vintners (then the largest agricultural co-op in California), had been given an assignment to "do something" about Cresta Blanca.

Cresta Blanca had been a major brand name in wine 30 years earlier but by this time had become almost moribund.

California is divided into two Alcohol Beverage Commission areas. Cresta Blanca had retail distribution in the northern district only. Competition for distribution of wine by the wholesalers and, more important, for store shelf space throughout the country, was intense. There was no available budget of sufficient size at Guild to enter this fray of competition for distribution.

Another company, Tiburon Vintners, now known as Windsor Vineyards, had at that time established a reputation for great success with their innovative wine-selling by mail.

Management decided to imitate Tiburon and sell Cresta Blanca wine by mail in Southern California. I studied the Tiburon mailing and wasn't at all impressed. In fact, I thought it was pretty poor. But I'm always swayed by numbers, and there were so many stories in the direct-mail industry extolling Tiburon's success that I had to pay attention.

The Tiburon promotion initially sold a sample case of two bottles of each of six different varietal wines. Tiburon then used follow-up mailings selling a special offer on one of the varietals.

Tiburon also did a big job selling wine in bottles with personalized labels, an item not available to us at Cresta Blanca.

Tiburon wasn't creating new wine drinkers but rather converting people from drinking jug wines like Ripple to varietal wines.

Test packages were written by Jack Walsh, Hank Burnett and Bill Jayme. In addition to the three originals, we prepared an imitation of the Tiburon package. The imitation was so close to the original that at a luncheon attended by all the major vintners, the Tiburon people complained to the president of Guild—who promised not to do it again.

As it happens, the packages of all three of our copywriters handily beat the Tiburon package imitation and the Burnett package brought in several times as many orders. The results enabled us to make a projection that we could sell 100,000 cases a year in Southern California. Believe me when I tell you that's a more than significant amount of wine.

Fulfillment, though, was a horror. Breakage ran so high that UPS refused to handle any further shipments. Instead of attempting to solve the shipping problem, the client killed the project. (This took place before the development of the Styrofoam cartons used today.)

As it happens, many small wineries in California, unable to get retail distribution, have in recent years turned to direct marketing by mail to sell their product successfully.

Herb Drake, after retiring from Guild, has kept his hand in the marketing of wine in a modest and most unusual way. He has a vast knowledge of the small wineries of California. As a result, he is able to purchase some superior wines in limited quantity. He then uses these rare vintages to conduct fund raising for causes such as the Stanford University alumni fund and the San Francisco Symphony.

Herb holds wine tastings with officers of the sponsoring group as well as some well-known wine experts, to choose the individual wine to be used. He also does a particularly good job of having special pictorial labels designed, which adds a certain amount of cachet to the promotion.

REDBOOK

Bob Farley retained us to help him market *Redbook* magazine. This was my third time around with Charter Magazines, having previously worked on circulation at *Ladies' Home Journal* and *American Home*. We had also worked with Charter on a continuity series of books after they moved to New York.

Redbook was doing a sweepstakes drawing. The magazine was about to start a new sweeps, intending to repeat the same prize structure they had used in their last contest. This is unusual, but the previous sweepstakes had been very successful and Redbook executives felt the prize structure had been an integral part of their success.

As it happened, the entry periods for the two sweeps overlapped. I had convinced Bob to change to a lucky number or a predrawn sweepstakes. Since we were able to mail both versions at the same time, we ended up with a perfect test of a drawing versus lucky number and the lucky number version had a 30% better response.

Psychologically it's much more difficult for the recipient to ignore and throw away a lucky number ticket that may already be a winner than to throw away an entry form that will be put in a drawing from which a winner is drawn.

In analyzing *Redbook's* renewal series, I noticed that cash-with-order for renewals was less than 25% compared to a rule-of-thumb standard for magazines of 50-55%. (At this point you should understand: *Redbook* and its sister publications had been through a number of cost-saving innovations.)

When I looked at the actual renewal mailing packages, I found that management, to save money, had removed the reply envelope from the package. I became an instant hero when I had them put the reply envelopes back in and cash-with-order renewals returned to the more normal 50% level.

PSYCHOLOGY TODAY

From a circulation standpoint, *Psychology Today* was a sensational success from its first issue. It's the only magazine in my 40 years of experience that could economically pick up new subscribers in large volume through space advertising. As a result of this well-publicized success, many magazines attempted to emulate *Psychology Today's* approach via the exchange of space advertising.

Except for those magazines that could run ads in their own pages—space that otherwise would have been used for editorial (i.e., magazines that carry only the minimum number of pages they're willing to deliver to the customer)—I've never since then found space advertising at any magazine to be a profitable source for generating substantial numbers of subscriptions. *American Heritage* in the early days was an exception in that it could successfully advertise with bind-in cards in large-circulation magazines like *Time* and *TV Guide*.

I think the reason *Psychology Today* was successful in its

space advertising for circulation was that no matter how we described the magazine, large numbers of people bought a subscription because they thought it would provide an instant lifestyle change. There are great numbers of unhappy people who want an easy answer to what's wrong with their lives.

At *Psychology Today*, I used what I called a Love Letter. This was the first time this concept was used anywhere, as far as a I know.

The Love Letter grew out of a promotion we first did at Time-Life when I worked there 40 years ago. Time had successfully been selling 39-week subscriptions in the acquisition mailings. The magazine then switched to a subscription with a 78-week term, also very successfully, but conversions of the 78-week subscriptions were at a substantially lower percentage.

One of the people in the creative department at *Time* wrote what was called a cultivation letter. This letter congratulated the reader upon being a subscriber, to *Time* and thus a member of a very elite group. It then went on to detail the demographics of a *Time* subscriber, which were indeed high in income and education.

The cultivation letter was mailed about halfway through the 78-week subscription and resulted in conversion percentages returning to the levels of the old 39-week offer. I don't know whether Time is still using this type of letter, but I saw one only a couple of years ago.

The Love Letter I did for *Psychology Today* was nothing more than a poster mailed in a tube with a cover letter. We told the subscriber we hoped he or she would enjoy the poster, which had been very popular with our advertising prospects. There was no offer or response device in the mailing package—hence the term "Love Letter." The letter was mailed just prior to the first conversion effort and had a more than justifiable effect on conversion percentage.

I've used the Love Letter concept successfully in a number of other situations. At Amoco, almost unbelievably, a decal for the car window saying, "I have been a member of Amoco Motor Club since [year]" lifted conversion response.

Psychology Today merchandised a book club which

certainly seemed a natural extension of the magazine. The club reached a membership of well over 150,000. In my experience, acquisition of book-club members has never been so easy as it was at *Psychology Today*. Members could be acquired for less than $1 plus the cost of the premium.

Despite this low cost of acquisition, the book club was never profitable. Bad pay for even the low-price premium package was a real problem. That may have been because the offer was too "soft." I do know that most clubs experience their biggest bad-pay difficulties on the initial package.

Perhaps an equally important factor in the failure of small book clubs, and *Psychology Today*'s in particular, is the insidious built-in growth of inventories. The inevitable day of reckoning comes when the inventories have to be written off. The result can be devastating.

During this period *Psychology Today* acquired the Limited Edition Book Club. John Tosarello, promotion director of the Limited Edition Book Club, had developed one of the truly unique and great one-shot mailing packages.

John's concept was to sell a suite of 29 original Picasso prints, published by Abrams. The selling price was $5,800. The mailing was packaged in a box measuring roughly 10"×10". Inside was a heavy three-panel brochure. One panel held several actual transparencies of the Picasso prints. Underneath this, cushioned in tissue paper, was the selling document and order form requesting a $1,000 deposit. The package was mailed first class and the cost of the package in the mail was $10 each.

Even at that cost, it was a profitable promotion. This is the only example I can remember of a mass promotion being mailed in a box.

While I personally don't particularly care for Picasso, I bought a set of the prints and for a number of years several of them hung in our home. Several years ago, I donated them to the Jacksonville, Florida, Art Museum. The museum held a special show of the prints. I have to admit that properly hung and lit, they were absolutely beautiful. Incidentally, their catalog value had increased to $15,000 by then.

SOUTHERN LIVING

Southern Living has been a client of mine for more than 20 years. They hired us in October 1965 and published their first issue the following February.

Prior to that, *Southern Living* had been an editorial section in *Progressive Farmer,* a magazine with a circulation of about one million. The people in this company had very little experience in direct mail.

Some years later Emory Cunningham, president of *Southern Living,* wrote about the day they hired me.

"My first time to see Richard Benson was when the board of directors of the Progressive Farmer Company held interviews during a meeting in Birmingham to select a circulation consultant. The decision had been made to launch *Southern Living* magazine in early 1966, and in the fall of 1965 the company was seeking a direct-mail authority to help with circulation acquisition for the new monthly.

"The first candidate for the consultant's job with our company was an impeccably dressed, smooth-talking, impressive young man from Chicago. His voice was like those you hear on the national network news each evening— melodious and pleasant to hear. He made a smooth, skillful presentation and departed the meeting.

"Then it was Dick Benson's turn. He came in, took a sort of disdainful look around the room, brushed a hand through his already rumpled hair and told us in a rather gruff way that the direct-mail business was an unusual business and we apparently knew very little about it.

"He was completely honest in telling our directors that we were confronted with a 180-degree about-face in circulation tactics... if *Southern Living* was to grow and be profitable circulation-wise. Within ten minutes, every director knew that if we selected Dick Benson as a consultant, three things would be certain: (1) We could depend on what he told us to be fact; (2) There would be times we would be exasperated with him because of his unbending demands for accuracy; and (3) That if anyone could help us to launch *Southern Living's* circulation program successfully, he was probably the man."

Time was too short for a preliminary test. The publishing company was establishing *Southern Living* by transferring to the new magazine the subscriptions of *Progressive Farmer* subscribers who lived in cities. Management wanted to generate an additional 50,000 subscriptions by mail.

I said we could do it. The saving grace was that charter subscriptions were priced at $1. We made an initial mailing of one million pieces and pulled 93,000 subscriptions. In the ensuing years, *Southern Living* grew and grew, far outstripping *Sunset* magazine, after which it had been patterned. Today it has well over two million subscribers.

The big thing my experience at *Southern Living* taught me, as a Yankee, was that a Southerner is a Southerner is a Southerner. Circulation-marketing was relatively easy at *Southern Living* because Southerners will more strongly support a Southern product produced by Southerners than will other regional populations. Southerners are Southerners and Texans are Texans, but most of the rest of us are simply Americans.

Unlike most magazines during those years, *Southern Living*, with our urging, was continually aggressive about circulation pricing, with the result that today a subscription sells for $20. Compare that $20 price to the price of other mass-circulation women's magazines. *Sunset* sells for only $12.95.

Southern Living has been totally direct-mail driven. It was built on semiannual sweepstakes mailings. Unlike the sweepstakes of other women's magazines, we had a new sweepstakes every six months. Since we also did a semi-annual advance renewal mailing using the sweepstakes, I didn't want to repeat the same sweepstakes six months later to the same audience.

For many years, our total prize structure was a modest $60,000 or so, often featuring a "second home" as the grand prize.

Southern Living's mailing packages were simpler and cost substantially less than those of other women's magazines for which I worked. The prize structure, too, was much lower than others offered. The percentage of households we mailed in *Southern Living's* Southern states region was at least as high as the penetration of the United States by the other major women's magazines. While it's difficult to make direct comparisons, by my analysis order-cost was substantially less at *Southern Living*. In my opinion, no little part of this success was due to a new sweepstakes prize structure with each mailing.

OXMOOR HOUSE

Southern Living's entry into the book-publishing business was highlighted by a number of early successes, particularly a book about the South titled *Jericho*. *Jericho* was written by James Dickey and illustrated by Hubert Shuptrine. It was an enormous success both in the mail and in bookstores.

In addition, Oxmoor House, *Southern Living's* book-publishing division, had a number of big-selling cookbooks... and a few failures, like a book on mushrooms.

Not many magazine publishers have established successful hard-cover book businesses. Oxmoor House has done very, very well. Unfortunately there were problems for a short period; in my opinion these occurred because the publisher of Oxmoor House became carried away with the idea of trade publishing, moving away from publishing primarily for mail-order sale to publishing for the trade (bookstores).

(It's the exception rather than the rule for a trade publisher to make profits from his current season's list of new books.)

The publisher of Oxmoor House optimistically set print orders larger than the quantities recommended by his marketing people. That old bugaboo, inventories, caught up with him.

It has always been my belief—probably based on my *American Heritage* experience—that magazine publishers who enter the book business should think of it as an *incremental* business. The publisher's inside edge is that he has a subscriber mailing list and a special ability to market to it. The decision to publish a given title should be based first on the results of a concept survey (discussed elsewhere) of subscribers and then further reinforced by a dry test to subscribers. Lacking these tests, one substantially increases the possibility of failure.

Some years ago, I encouraged *Southern Living* to get into the annual book business. The concept of the annual business is this: When the customer signs up to buy his first book he agrees that in succeeding years the annual book will be automatically shipped and billed. The customer does have the opportunity to cancel the arrangement at any time.

Oxmoor House's first major success in annuals was a hardcover book containing all the recipes published in *Southern Living* during the previous year, with an index.

The business of annuals at *Southern Living* now contributes a very significant share of the empire's publishing profits.

Time Inc. bought *Southern Living* a couple of years ago, with the result that in a roundabout way, I am working for Time Inc. once again.

8
CREDIT CARDS, BIBLES AND A LITTLE SPANISH TOWN

AMERICAN EXPRESS

I had worked on the American Express account when I was consulting with Ogilvy & Mather. At Benson Associates, I again had American Express as an account.

Our most exciting assignment for American Express was to introduce the sale of merchandise charged to the travel card. This was a start-up business for them.

Our responsibility was total—searching out the original merchandise products and preparing the promotion mailings American Express sent to cardholders. Merchandise ran the gamut from expensive novelties to electronics and appliances. Perhaps our most unusual early success was the promotion of a grandfather clock.

After our initial efforts, American Express went on to establish an internal department for selling merchandise by mail. This department has built a major business and profit stream.

While we had absolutely nothing to do with it, it's worth mentioning that American Express at a later date had the most successful one-shot mailing ever done by anyone. With the Franklin Mint as their partner, they sold the "One Hundred Great Books," leather-bound, at $28 each. That's a $2,800 commitment on the part of the customer! I heard the promotion produced some 30,000 orders—more than $85 million in sales from a single promotional mailing.

I love "street stories." One was that the Franklin Mint, in order to hedge the future cost of leather, had purchased a goat farm in Spain. I have no idea whether the story is true, but I can't find anybody to deny it.

NEW YORK MAGAZINE

New York magazine was one of the early "city" magazines.

We were retained to help with the circulation launch. Bill Jayme wrote a marvelous package incorporating a sweepstakes. The concept of the prize structure was of Bill's own making. The first prize included an evening with John Lindsay, the very popular mayor of New York. The ploy that helped to make Bill's sweepstakes so successful was his consolation prize—a one-way ticket to Los Angeles.

The launch of *New York* exceeded all subscription expectations. George Hirsch, the publisher, decided the magazine wouldn't need additional direct mail for the next two years. So three months after publication George fired us from the account.

Several years later, Clay Felker, editor and CEO of *New York*, again retained us to help launch *New West*, their new magazine in California. Once again, the launch far exceeded projections of circulation.

I must be a slow learner. Again they fired us about three months after they began publication.

ROSENFELD, SIROWITZ AND LAWSON

One of the major projects we worked on for the advertising agency Rosenfeld, Sirowitz and Lawson was for a subsidiary of Citibank. We created mailings intended to increase the acquisition of applications for second-mortgage loans.

Initial results from our test mailings showed dramatic improvement over the previous control packages, and the new package was rolled out in monthly mailings. Total applications were double the previous results. But when final numbers became available, the net made loans were no better than from the previous mailings.

Our early research showed there was no real difference in either the quality of the lists mailed or in the quality of the applications received. So what was wrong?

The problem wasn't in the mailings. We learned that the people responsible for approving loan applications had monthly application-approval quotas. When they reached their quotas for the month, they rejected the rest of the applications, no matter how qualified the applicants might be.

There were no medals for individuals exceeding their quotas, but there was trouble for approving an application if the loan turned bad. As is true of so many people everywhere, "safe" was the only way to go.

Once discovered, the problem was solved and the new mailings continued. Here's what we learned from this series of mailings:

MARKETING IS ONLY AS GOOD AS THE SUPPORTING INFRASTRUCTURE.

THE AMERICAN BIBLE SOCIETY

The major purpose of the American Bible Society was to distribute individual books of the Bible, translated into a vast number of languages, to people in countries all over the world—including those behind the Iron Curtain.

This was my first fund-raising-by-mail client. Since I knew nothing about the field, my thinking wasn't inhibited by past experience.

The mailing we developed for the Bible Society was written by Jack Walsh. It broke a great deal of new ground in fund raising. I'll tell you how:

Fund raisers in general almost always ask for money in specific alternative amounts or whatever you can give. To my knowledge, they had never used credit or a "bill me" option in the mail.

Up to the time of our program, the average donation to the Bible Society was less than $5. My plan was to ask only for a pledge, with no fall-back request for "cash now." I chose to ask for a $2 monthly pledge. Why? Because that is cash money and doesn't require a check or money-order decision.

Jack Walsh created a wonderful package built around a token depicting a mountain and the line, "Only faith can move mountains. Start with this one."

The idea for a pledge came from a fact I had learned: Seventy percent of the money pledged by the viewers of the first fund-raising telethons was actually collected. This despite the fact most of the small donors—some of whom were children—made their pledges just to get their names on the television screen.

Our mailing was a huge success, but for some never-explained reason the Society was against it and decided not to go ahead with additional mailings. After only three months they fired us.

My impression was that either the management of the Bible Society thought $2 donors were a waste of time (not an uncommon thought in fund-raising circles) or the success was such that they felt there had to be something wrong (possibly moral).

Sometime afterward, the net numbers apparently caused them to change their minds. They rolled out with the package, then continued to mail it. Several years later Ed Mayer, their consultant, told me they then had 250,000 people contributing $2 a month.

The fulfillment package we had designed for the people who gave us a pledge consisted of a thank-you letter, a newsletter detailing the activities of the Bible Society for the previous three months, and three dated pledge-reply envelopes. Every three months, a new letter would go out to donors telling what had been done with the contributors' money and what work was planned for the next period, for which the Bible Society needed their continued contributions. Again, three dated reply envelopes were included as well as a "soft" dunning message if the contributor were delinquent in keeping up with his pledge.

DOW JONES

The *Wall Street Journal* was beyond any doubt the oddest account I've ever worked with. Testing was nonexistent, with the possible exception of lists; and even they weren't done well.

The *Wall Street Journal* was so successful and made so much money that no one really thought or cared about the efficiency or economics of circulation. If management wanted more circulation, the circulation department's answer was, "Just give us the money."

The publication mailed monthly in big volume—not because the circulation department was taking advantage of fresh hotline names (this was before hotlines, as we know them, were readily available), but because, since these people had their own fulfillment department, they wanted to spread the work on a monthly basis in order to balance the workload.

Before we came along, executives at the *Journal* weren't aware that in some months their order costs were six times the cost of the best mailing months. Nor did they care.

We didn't get them to give up monthly mailings, but we did manage to get them to mail much higher volume in the good months. It was at The *Wall Street Journal* that I first learned that an incentive for a cash order isn't economically efficient. All my tests since then have proved out this truism. At the time the *Journal's* offer was 11 weeks for $5, with two extra weeks added to your subscription if you enclosed cash.

The *Journal* was very happy with this offer because it brought in 80% cash with the order.

Now, here's my premise: The customer perceives an incentive for cash as an increase in price for credit and therefore a penalty for credit. The buyer feels his 30-day credit is as good as cash, so if he isn't willing to pay cash he doesn't order at all because of what he perceives to be a higher price.

I suggested we test a subscription of 13 weeks for cash or credit. We mailed a test and pulled only 50% cash with order, but 40% more total orders came in—a net order count of 122 compared to every 95 orders previously.

The *Wall Street Journal* had one of the longest-running control packages I have ever known. The letter started off: "Who, me? Yes, you." It had been in use for more than 20 years, millions and millions of pieces of mail. Its longevity was exceeded only by the *Barron's* "widow" package which began mailing prior to World War II and was still mailing not very long ago.

Several times we had mailing packages created by some of the best freelance writers. None was able to beat the *Journal's* control copy. But we did substantially improve the results from the control package by making some changes.

For example: A very substantial improvement in The *Wall Street Journal's* response resulted from changing their labeled closed-face envelope to a labeled order card showing through a window in the envelope. And the addition of the simulated typewritten name of the signer of the letter over the envelope corner card increased orders substantially.

The *Journal* mailings illustrated another point that became a basic principle for me and was proven to be true elsewhere:

CONTRARY TO POPULAR OPINION, WE FOUND NO DIFFERENCE IN RESULTS IN ADDRESSING BY TITLE AS COMPARED TO ADDRESSING BY NAME.

I should add that the success of *The Wall Street Journal*, during the years I followed the situation, was a wonderful illustration of the importance of a great product and how it could overcome mediocre promoters.

TOURIST COMMISSION OF SPAIN

The Tourist Commission of Spain gave me an assignment I welcomed: the development of a mailing package selling a 15-day tour of Spain.

The final mailing package illustrates once again how broad are the parameters of products that can be sold by mail. This was in 1972, and the price of the trip was $514-$599. The trip included some unique ingredients including being knighted. The letter, written by Jack Walsh, follows. (To gather the material for the letter, I did much of the tour by going to Spain for four days.)

El Presidente de la Comisión
de Promoción y Publicidad
Turística de La Mancha

Dear Reader: Soon, perhaps very soon, you're going to go away again. Maybe you're thinking of spending a great deal of money going to where you've been before or perhaps some new place you hope will be worth the risk.

If this is the case, I think you'll be glad you received this letter and even more glad if you accept its invitation. If you do accept...

you'll spend 15 days in one of the most enchanting areas of the world—La Mancha, Spain—for just $514,* complete.

"Complete" means just that. Except for shopping money and enough to pay for dinner the nights you're in Madrid (we'll describe ten to 12 fine restaurants and let you choose by your own tastes), you don't even need to have tip money with you.

You will return as a knight with a replica of the sword you were ordered with and diploma signed by the mayor of Puerto Lapice—the same village where Don Quixote was knighted.

La Mancha is, of course, the impossible dreamland of Don Quixote and as the guest of my province of Ciudad Real you shall explore it with just 39 other fortunate vacationers as it has never been explored before.

The limit of only 40 people is, I think you'll agree, a prudent one. Enough people of like interests for you to make several new friends during your 15-day excursion, yet not so many that you are treated like a member of an oversubscribed charter flight.

But let me start at the beginning. And that's aboard a luxurious Iberia Airlines of Spain 747, or any other regular carrier, as it departs from John F. Kennedy Airport in New York. After six hours of spacious comfort, delicious meals and a feature-length movie, you'll set down in beautiful Madrid—the ancient capital of Spain.

Here you'll stay for three relaxing days at the Hotel Don Quixote, appropriately enough, where you'll relax, shop and get acquainted with your fellow passengers. There will be a grand sightseeing tour that will afford you special entrée to spectacular Prado Museum and Royal Palace.

At about 3:00 p.m. on the fourth day, you'll take a 26-kilometer, air-conditioned excursion to Alcalá de Henares to visit Cervantes' home and the University. Before you return to Madrid, you'll enjoy a wonderful meal at the Student Inn and a 30-minute slide show which will familiarize you with the La Mancha you are about to explore.

And from there on in it's a stimulating, well-paced adventure through the land where windmills were jousted and ideals were conjured ... and where you'll create lifetime memories.

For instance, the very next day—the fifth—you will visit:

Ocaña—a town that boasts jewels of authentic Castilian architecture, revitalizing hot springs and thermal baths.

Tembleque—a staggering example of unrestored

Castilian architecture, giving an immediate comparison to the restored Ocaña structures.

Campo de Criptana—where you will contribute a stone to the building of the Windmill of Peace and receive a document certifying that you participated.

El Toboso—where the naming of Dulcinea's Order (Sweetheart's Order) will take place and diplomas will be distributed to every lady present.

Mota del Cuervo—checking in at the Mesón of Don Quixote, you'll be met by hosts representing the Quixote and Sancho Panza and after dinner (served with lilting regional music), you'll visit artisans at work making pottery.

On the sixth day, you'll progress to Cuenca (through three lovely villages, which you'll visit briefly) where you'll spend the evening and *participate in a free raffle of a painting of the Modern Art Museum.*

The seventh day takes you to Albacete, one of the most "see-worthy" towns in all of Spain. You'll visit the Provincial Archeological Museum, the Church of Nuestra Señora de la Asunción, a local cutlery factory and many more places of interest.

The next day you'll go to Valdepeñas ... via Alcaraz, Osa de Montiel, Ruidera, Tomelloso, Argamasilla de Alba. The last is where Cervantes wrote his masterpiece and you'll be treated to a "light and sound" performance—an inkwell-and-feathers allegory of Don Quixote scriptures.

From Valdepeñas, you'll go to Puerto Lapice. On the way, you'll visit Santa Cruz de Mudela (to practice bullfighting if you like).

At Valdepeñas, one of the wine centers of the world, you'll be presented with three bottles of superb Spanish wine and an authentic wineskin.

You'll proceed to Ciudad Real, where you will have lunch at Los Castillos Hotel, (one "must" here is the Casa Consistorial with its beautiful Greek-Roman facade). On the way you'll visit Almagro (where you'll see a special comedy presentation—you will be also able to show your talent as an actor, and watch world-famous embroiderers at work). That night will be spent in Puerto Lapice.

> Here the knighting will take place. You'll be given a diploma signed by the mayor after the following words are recited over you: "I name you Knight so that your noble wishes may be fulfilled in the name of God and the King." Knighthood, of course, symbolizes perhaps better than any custom ever devised man's noble ideals ... perfection for himself, justice for his fellow man, love for everyone. And the next day in Toledo, you'll be presented with a one-foot replica of the sword that knighted you which I believe you'll be proud to display the rest of your life.

At ten the next morning you leave for Toledo ... a city that is unique unto itself, and if you've ever seen El Greco's masterpiece you will understand why.

On the way, in Consuegra, you'll be presented with a small sack of flour, "The Flour of Peace," which will be one more proud memento of this inspiring journey. Dinner in Toledo will be hosted by an official representative of the city, who will distribute the sword replicas. And after a delicious meal you'll be invited on a walking tour of the city, which will be magnificently lighted for the occasion.

The next morning you'll see the city in daylight—visiting the Cathedral, the Church of San Tomé which houses El Greco's famous painting *El Entierro del Conde de Orgaz*, the Sinagoga del Tránsito, El Greco's House and Museum and the Museum Hospital of Santa Cruz.

After lunch you'll reluctantly leave Toledo for Madrid—going through Esquivias, Illescas and Calzada. When the two-hour drive is over, you'll be checking in once again at Hotel Don Quixote.

The twelfth day will take you to some of Madrid's most famous landmarks: the Monastery of El Escorial, some 30 miles from the city, with the Basílica, Salas Capitulares, Panteón de los Reyes, the Palace Library and the private rooms of King Philip II. Lunch at the Hotel Felipe II will be followed by a trip to the Valley of the Fallen, which commemorates the dead of the Spanish Civil War and is an arresting piece of modern architecture.

The thirteenth and fourteenth days are yours to do with as you choose, and I suggest you devote part of it to shopping in Madrid's many and inexpensive shops. Lace, pottery, embroidery work are distinctive and low-priced . . . and they make wonderful gifts for those who will be waiting at home to hear about your great adventure in La Mancha.

As much fun and excitement as this adventure promises to be, I think you'd agree that it would be more fun if you had recently read *Don Quixote* before departure. Accordingly, we will send you a gold-stamped, handsomely bound hardcover copy of this remarkable volume as soon as you say you'd like to come along. It's among the best 940 pages in modern literature and a permanent enhancement to your bookshelf.

There isn't much more to say. The enclosed folder tells you more about the trip, but no one could tell you everything. You know the price—just

$514.* If you're a frequent traveller, you perhaps know that's not even $190 more than the 14-day excursion fare alone.

Actually, the only thing to say is: Please tell us you'll come. Doing so is as easy as returning the enclosed form in the postpaid envelope provided.

Do it now, please. I have a feeling those 40 seats are going to be occupied very quickly and we must honor reservations on a first come, first serve basis.

Espero tener la grata oportunidad de su respuesta.

Atentamente,

José María Aparicio Arce

* For high-season departures (June, July, August), price slightly increased to $599.

MCGRAW-HILL

McGraw-Hill is the publisher of *Business Week* magazine. The company retained us to help them launch a new publication, the *Business Week Newsletter*. We did this quite successfully but mostly in a traditional manner.

I felt *Business Week* itself illustrated two no-no's in the magazine's promotion for new subscriptions. We had suggested they test a less-than-one-year offer to acquire new subscribers. My experience has shown that initial eight-month subscribers convert or buy the second time at the same rate as first-time subscribers who have bought for one year—and you get more response per thousand pieces mailed. The management of *Business Week* magazine was adamant. They wouldn't sell subscriptions for less than one year. They wouldn't even test.

In my opinion, it's foolish not to test something a number of people find successful, even if you feel you won't want to implement the results. I believe you should test and bank the information you get. It may well be that the financial success of a test will change your preformed opinion.

Some years later, the management of *Business Week* changed its mind and did move to selling introductory subscriptions for less than one year. On one occasion *Business Week* skipped its semiannual summer mailing because of the common fixation by public companies on fiscal year profits—which were down and would be "further negatively influenced by a promotion mailing."

THE RESULTS ILLUSTRATE WHY A REGULAR SEMIANNUAL MAILING SHOULD NOT BE PASSED EVEN IF YOU MAIL A REDUCED QUANTITY AND ONLY THE MORE PROFITABLE PORTION OF YOUR MAILING UNIVERSE.

Sure enough, when the new year came, *Business Week,* in order to make the circulation advertising rate-base guarantee, was forced to mail all the way through April. Because of the extra mail and the poorer mailing season, they paid as much as four times their normal cost for subscription acquisition.

MAILING LISTS DO NOT SHOW MUCH BETTER RESULTS MAILED WITH A YEAR'S REST THAN WITH SIX MONTHS' REST.

You can see how the principles start to pile up when you have the results of enough mailings at your elbow. More coming up.

9
NEWSPAPER, NEWS MAGAZINE, SALE OF BENSON, STAGG AND MORE

THE *CHRISTIAN SCIENCE MONITOR*

Everybody knows the *Christian Science Monitor,* the national newspaper published in Boston.

We developed a successful promotion for acquiring new subscribers to the *Monitor.* But their fulfillment department was a total mess, and more than three months went by before service started on a new subscription. Contrast this to next-day delivery by the *Wall Street Journal.*

The result was that bad pay and cancellations were incredibly high. Top management wasn't willing to face up to doing something about the core of the problem: a long-time manager who wasn't producing.

The *Monitor* terminated our relationship when I suggested it was foolish to spend promotion money attracting new subscribers if the fulfillment department couldn't handle the business.

A year later, the publication terminated the consultant who succeeded us with the words, "Benson was right. Unless and until we straighten out our fulfillment department, we shouldn't continue to promote new subscriptions."

It's nice to be right, but often it isn't very profitable.

The fact is that mine was the right advice. I've never worried about the personal consequences even if it meant losing the account.

Here we are 15 years later. I've just learned the *Christian Science Monitor* is closing down its fulfillment department and is moving the function to an outside service company.

U.S. NEWS & WORLD REPORT

U.S. News & World Report is a newsweekly published in Washington, D.C.

U.S. News was my client on two different occasions. The people at *U.S. News* with whom I had contact had all worked together for years. There was an atmosphere of an Ivy League gentlemen's club whose members never argued with one another and never raised any issue that might cause dissension. They felt they did everything well, they did it differently, and their way was the only way to manage circulation for *U.S. News*.

The business manager and the circulation people resisted change, particularly if it might cause disagreements within the group. When tokens on order cards came into vogue we dragged—and I do mean dragged—the *U.S. News* people into making a test. The addition of a token to the order card was a success, but the creative director didn't feel it was "appropriate" for *U.S. News*. A token with a new design by the creative director was tested and again it was a winner.

TOKENS OR STICKERS ON ORDER CARDS WILL ALMOST ALWAYS INCREASE RESPONSE.

Once again, the creative director felt the tokens weren't "appropriate" and insisted on still another token design and a new test. The creative director proved his point: The test failed.

U.S. News had literally designed the token out of existence; to make sure, the creative director manipulated this last design in a manner that all but guaranteed its failure. It was virtually impossible to put the token in the provided slot.

So far as I know, tokens were never heard of again at *U.S. News*.

During one of my terms at *U.S. News,* a new product called the *U.S. News Letter* was started. The magazine itself contained five so-called newsletters but this separate publication was to be boldly different. The premise for the new publication was that it would deal more in rumors and predictions, which the editors wouldn't be able to use in the magazine.

The newsletter would stick its neck out and forecast what the president or Congress or whoever would do regarding various current issues. If the predictions turned out to be wrong, the editors would admit it and go on. Hope was that the editor's batting average would be good.

The premise was sound. If memory serves me, *U.S. News Letter* built a circulation of some 100,000. The editorial premise wasn't fulfilled; in fact, I can't tell you why any of the material used in the newsletter wasn't suitable for the magazine. The letter did not stick its neck out and make predictions.

After a few years, the newsletter died as a separate publication and I'd guess its inevitable death came about because it had no unique quality.

The *U.S. News* executives considered the choice and purchase of lists for their promotions as a function not worthy of their personal involvement. The list function was turned over to a clerk, who in turn relied completely on list brokers (the prevailing policy in far too many companies). The result was that for a company with so large a volume of mail, *U.S. News* undoubtedly did the poorest job of list usage I've witnessed.

Some time later *U.S. News* turned the function of scheduling lists and list selection over to the Kleid Co. Kleid did a much better job of list selection and scheduling; in fact, the Kleid Co., under Rose Harper, not only performs this function well for a number of companies, but also is a fine list-broker in the traditional manner.

In spite of Kleid's doing a better job and in spite of my deep-rooted convictions about buying around the corner, I think generally putting the list function out-of-house is a major error. No mailer should be that far removed from this essential function.

I KNOW OF NO MAILER WHO SPENDS ENOUGH TIME ON LISTS.

For a number of years, *U.S. News* published "coffee table" picture books.

A new "dry test" promotion mailing became a rollout control mailing for several different book projects. This mailing had no brochure, even though these were lavish picture books! It was built on the premise that an idea for a new product had come across the publisher's desk and before acting on it, he wanted to know how the subscriber felt about it. The mailing went on to ask for the order.

This copy platform is successful because it's believable. People like to be asked for advice; they become insiders, and everybody wants to be an insider.

I had had the same type of copy work for me with a new continuity series at Oxmoor House, the book-publishing arm of *Southern Living*.

For several months toward the end of my second term with *U.S. News*, I tried to get the publication to rent its subscription lists. At the time, *U.S. News* was a company with $100 million gross sales and a tiny net profit of possibly $2 million. It doesn't take much of a jiggle in costs to wipe out such a small profit.

I estimated conservatively that list-rental income would net $500,000 the first year and grow to at least $1 million a year. In fact, I felt that if the company would at least exchange lists with other publishers whose lists they used, the savings in annual promotion costs would be at least $250,000.

My first meeting ever was set up with John Sweet, the CEO of *U.S. News*. Mr. Sweet was primed for me and immediately proceeded to lecture me for 15 minutes on "the special relationship of *U.S. News* with its subscribers." List rental just was "not appropriate" to the way *U.S. News* treated its readers.

I wasn't supposed to know the *U.S. News* profit-and-loss figures, but I managed to get Mr. Sweet to discuss them. I then proceeded to pontificate: "It seems to me the first responsibility of a publisher, who has an editorial point of view he wants to promulgate, is to be sure he makes a profit so he can continue to publish."

My argument didn't win the day and at the end of the meeting I went downstairs to the general manager's office and resigned.

One way or another, straight talk has often lost me the account; or when they wouldn't listen I've resigned the account.

Two weeks later Mr. Sweet relented and *U.S. News* put its subscription list on the market. But I never again worked for *U.S. News*.

THE SALE OF BENSON, STAGG, AND ASSOCIATES, INC.

In 1969, I sold Benson, Stagg and Associates, Inc., to Republic, Inc. Republic was the old Roy Rogers movie company, and was listed on the New York Stock Exchange.

I had grown up as an avid reader of Horatio Alger, whose books were always about the newspaper boy who through hard work became a man by making a million dollars. The stories always ended at that point and never went on to discuss what he then did with the money. My goal had always been to *make* a million dollars—not to have a million dollars.

When Republic offered me $920,000 worth of their treasury stock, that was close enough to a million and I sold the company. As it turned out, the sale was a disaster. By the time I was able to sell my stock, I received only $40,000. Republic stock was the biggest loser on the stock exchange in 1970-71, dropping in price from $92 to $4.

Six months after the sale, I resigned from Benson, Stagg over a question of ethics in the way I was being asked to conduct business. Not everybody loves me, but no one can say I ever purposely jabbed them—and I wasn't about to start doing so under corporate direction. This resignation, under the terms of my sale, cost me half the purchase price.

Shortly afterward I formed a partnership for direct-mail advertising with Lester Wunderman's agency, Wunderman, Ricotta & Kline. We did it on a trial basis, and it didn't take too long to show me I was no longer cut out to work in a structured corporate atmosphere. I had become too accustomed to making all the decisions myself, without consultation or thought about how it affected the business of others.

Before leaving Wunderman, I was instrumental in helping him purchase the Chapman division of Grey Advertising. This purchase worked out particularly well, and the Chapman subsidiary went on to become what is now a very large agency.

After leaving Wunderman in 1971, I began my consulting practice, which continues today. Before leaving the subject of Benson, Stagg, I have to mention the roster of great people who worked there.

—Dick Archer, who became creative head of Columbia House and a very good moonlighting copywriter.

—Dick Browner, a very talented art director who now runs his own shop.

—Hank Burnett, one of the truly great freelance copywriters and a fine, fine gentleman.

—Dick Leventer, now subscription director for all the Hearst magazines.

—Ed Mayer: A wonderful man and a superb teacher.

—Betty Ann Noakes, who went on to be a successful free-lance consultant.

—Jim Prendergast, a gentleman everybody loves, who established his own successful agency, which he sold to a major 4A agency ... and then later bought it back.

—Chris Stagg, who went on to be a very successful writer and consultant.

—Phyllis Stagg, who now heads her own successful agency.

—John Suhler, who became president of CBS magazines and now is president of the investment banker firm Veronis & Suhler, specializing in the media business.

I do want to thank them; they all made me look good.

HARPER'S MAGAZINE

Harper's magazine was a client of mine three different times. *Harper's* and the *Atlantic Monthly* were close competitors, editorially very similar; but the *Atlantic Monthly* sold twice as many copies for use in school classrooms. One of our early assignments was to do something about *Harper's* classroom sale.

We mounted a major campaign. The promotion was a total failure and I have never again tried to promote a consumer magazine for classroom use. I'm convinced that there is no economical method to make such a promotion work. I never understood (and as far as I know neither did anyone else understand) the disparity of classroom sale between the *Atlantic* and *Harper's*.

Harper's was in sad financial straits in those days, and there was little money for promotion. One mailing we developed showed promise and is one I repeated successfully at another magazine. We wrote to a list of prospects offering them a free introductory subscription. We then promoted them with our normal conversion series. We found a four-issues-free subscription to be more cost-effective than a three-issues-free offer.

Conversions of free introductory subscriptions to paid renewals were about 40% of our normal conversion percentage.

3M COMPANY

A leading direct-mail consultant, who had assisted several Fortune 500 companies with getting into direct mail, was retained by 3M to help them enter the publishing business.

The people at 3M told me their consultant had investigated more than 50 projects before selecting a continuity book series from Marshall Cavendish, the British publishers. The series was called *Contemporary Cooking* and was primarily about dinner-party cooking.

At our first meeting, the 3M people told me they had been promoting the series for more than a year, had spent more than $2 million, and still didn't have a successful mailing package or a proven universe of mailing lists. They were now budgeted and committed to make a two-million-piece mailing.

For the first hour or more of our initial meeting I attempted to dissuade them from hiring me and to persuade them instead to take their lumps and close the operation down. I pointed out: "Dinner-party entertaining has become generally outmoded with most women joining the job market. Women in general just don't have the time or energy for dinner parties."

My proposal to close down the operation was unacceptable.

Since there was no control package or proven list universe, I was starting from scratch, mailing the largest test mailing in history—two million pieces. Every test panel of the mailing was a failure. The operation was closed down several months later.

After the series closed down, I learned that a prime impetus for the program had been the opportunity to use "counter-trade" for the manufacture of the books. A simple explanation of counter-trade is barter. 3M could sell its regular products in Yugoslavia but had to accept product in payment. The books were produced there with funds which could not leave the country.

THIS DEMONSTRATES THE ADVISABILITY OF CONCEPT SURVEYS AND DRY TESTS (AS DESCRIBED ELSEWHERE). MOST OF THE LOSS IN-CURRED BY 3M WOULD HAVE BEEN AVOIDED WITH THE USE OF THESE SIMPLE DEVICES.

The 3M experience also shows the futility of trying to market a product when the public doesn't perceive it to be valuable.

MERRICO

Merrico is the bakery division of Anheuser-Busch and is the third-largest bakery in the country. The company retained me to help start a mail-order business selling fruitcake.

To appreciate this story, you have to understand: Their management thinks in terms of tonnage, not fruitcakes or even number of dollars.

THIS STORY ABOUT MERRICO IS AN ILLUS-TRATION OF WHY YOU NEED TO UNDERSTAND WHEN TO MAKE OR BUY.

The Merrico mail-order managers came to see me after the first holiday season for which I'd consulted on their mailings. Looking over the results, I could find no lettershop costs for the 250,000-piece test mailing. I asked them about it. They answered, "There were no costs."

Why? Headquarters personnel had sat around the office and inserted the mail by hand, because they didn't know about lettershops.

Since the business was a start-up and small, we arranged for them to do their mail-order recordkeeping with TABS.

TABS is a computer operation in Texas specializing in catalog work. If we hadn't done this, I doubt Merrico would ever have had the statistics necessary to make future marketing decisions for mail order.

By the third year, tests had made it clear that the only viable way to sell fruitcake was to include an actual slice in the acquisition mailings. We did this to the tune of one million slices.

While they were very thin slices, I suspect we used more fruitcake in the acquisition mailings than we sold to the customers.

Merrico's total fruitcake volume by mail was a tiny business by Anheuser-Busch standards, and small even by standards. It produced only a tiny profit. I asked why they really wanted to spend time on it and was told, "Mr. Busch wants to be in the mail-order business."

I'm not aware of their extending the product line since then or their acquiring other mail-order businesses, but if your name is Busch you can do anything you want. They continue to sell fruitcake by mail.

PIEDMONT PLANT

Piedmont Plant is a unique family business selling vegetable plants by mail. The third-generation young man, my initial contact, was an attractive fellow who had been a philosophy major in college and had studied language in Italy.

He now had returned to the family business and was to coin a phrase, a red dirt farmer. But he is a bright young man, and the business is certainly an interesting one.

At first blush, I'm sure you would have agreed with my initial doubts as to whether anything could be done to sell vegetable plants by mail. (I didn't know at that point that they had been in business for many years.)

When I joined them, the major share of Piedmont's business came from small farmers, but volume was going down as the number of small farmers continued to dwindle. A mailing was developed with a new approach: selling plants to a new market—home gardeners. The mailing consisted of a small catalog enclosed in an envelope along with a letter and an extra order card.

The mailing was quite successful. By about the third year (remember, these are annual promotions), we had a working package and a sizable proven list universe. At this point I felt we were in a position to take a giant step forward.

(As an aside, it might interest you to know that onions were the single largest sales volume items.)

I had presented my recommendations to the senior member of the firm. For an hour afterward our discussion went all around the subject without facing it. Finally he turned to me and said, "Mr. Benson, I don't know how I can lay an additional 8,000 orders on my office staff. They are my two older sisters."

We worked out an arrangement with BASS in Montgomery, Alabama, to handle the orders and prepare packing and shipping orders. This arrangement worked out quite well.

THIS IS JUST ONE MORE EXAMPLE OF MY "MAKE OR BUY" PHILOSOPHY.

Piedmont is still uncomfortable with the small order size from the home gardener compared to those from small farmer. On the other hand, up to now no one has found a efficient way to acquire small-farmer customers, and Piedmont is maintaining or increasing its gross sales.

10
MORE
MAGAZINES,
CONTEST
NEWS-LETTER,
COLLECTOR'S
PLATES

CHILDREN'S TELEVISION WORKSHOP

Children's Television Workshop produces *Sesame Street, The Electric Company* and other television shows. It also is a major publisher of magazines for children.

The head of the publishing division at Children's Television Workshop is Nina Link. Nina is bright, intelligent, innovative and blessed with boundless energy. What an edge this combination of traits gives the company!

Children's magazines are probably the most difficult category of magazines in which to make a profit. No matter how good your product, your readers are quickly growing out of their interest in your magazine.

My work at CTW has resulted in some improved results, but is also littered with a number of flops. A sweepstakes for *Sesame Street* proved to be a total failure.

(This is one of no more than five instances I can remember in which sweepstakes didn't improve the results. The others were *Psychology Today, Art in America, Smithsonian* and Columbia Record Club. I think I know what happened at *Art in America.* All our prizes were Picasso art objects, and Picasso isn't universally desirable. I have no rational explanation as to why the other sweepstakes didn't work.)

With an eye to expanding her subscriber base Nina Link started a parenting newsletter. With CTW as "authority" and what appeared to be an excellent product, I can't tell you why the newsletter wasn't a success.

At my behest, CTW tried an annual. Annuals are tremendously successful for encyclopedias, and *Southern Living* has also built an enormous volume with them. The "until forbid" contract with automatic shipment and the general inertia of the public contribute mightily to the success of annuals. Nevertheless, the annual was a failure at CTW.

When personal computers first became popular, Nina conceived of a computer magazine, *Enter,* for children. *Enter* had a very successful launch and appeared to be a winner. Unlike CTW's other magazines, though, *Enter* was dependent on advertising. When computer advertising everywhere fell away to almost nothing, *Enter,* along with a vast number of other computer magazines, was forced to close down.

List segmentation in the form of zip-penetration analysis currently appears to be the key to the future success of the other CTW magazines.

CTW has been aggressive in price testing. This enables them to continue to be viable even with the inroads of inflation on their costs.

Almost from the beginning of my tenure at CTW, I've pressed them to find new products to sell so that they can capitalize on their customer list. Despite the failures of the newsletter, the annual and *Enter*, they continue to pursue this goal. We have had success in selling a continuity series from another publisher, and there's no doubt in my mind we'll find other products to sell profitably to the customers of CTW. Nina Link—who is very open to ideas and, more important, is herself so very able—will see to it that CTW continues to be successful.

People like Nina make the difference in a company's chance for success.

CONTEST NEWS-LETTER

Contest News-Letter is a classic story of mail-order success started on a kitchen table. It also illustrates the fact that if you have a good idea, and persistence, and maybe a little bit of luck, you can still make your fortune in America.

Roger and Carolyn Tyndall were avid contest entrants when they decided to start their own newsletter. It wasn't an original idea; other contest letters were in the marketplace. In fact, one of them dates from the 1930s. The Tyndalls just felt they could do it better.

At the time, Roger was an air-traffic controller. He held that job until he was fired by President Reagan at the time of the controllers' strike. Carolyn worked at the local post office. They had won some prizes in contests and sweepstakes. (They still win prizes and as of this writing have won more than 200.)

The newsletter was started as a part-time business in 1974. Bill Capps, circulation director of *Southern Living*, saw an announcement of its start. We both laughed at the "dumb idea." Bill sent off for a sample copy; neither of us was impressed.

In 1974, I moved to Amelia Island, Florida, where, unbeknownst to me, Roger and Carolyn lived. At the time, I drove a Rolls Royce Silver Cloud and when they asked around, "Who is that driving the Silver Cloud?" the Tyndalls discovered I was a direct-mail consultant. Was it my reputation or the Rolls? They called me twice and tried to interest me in consulting for their letter. I told them to go away—they were too small and couldn't afford me.

One day, while I was out walking, the Tyndalls came by on their bicycles. At the side of the road we discussed their newsletter. They conducted the whole business from their house.

Contest News-Letter ran 12 pages. The printer had no binding equipment, so the Tyndalls folded the newsletter on their kitchen table, inserted it in the envelopes and mailed it themselves. They did all of their own fulfillment. And of course they researched and wrote the letter. Essentially, they operated out of a shoebox and ignored the fact that they were building a liability for future copies owed to subscribers. All this was the exact reverse of my "make or buy" philosophy. I still had no interest in their project.

The Tyndalls then told me how they had obtained an editorial plug in *Changing Times* magazine, which included an offer of a free issue if the reader sent a request containing a self-addressed stamped envelope. Know how many requests for sample copies this plug brought in? Ten thousand.

They mailed the sample copies; the newsletter had a price of $8 for one year (ten issues). The newsletter included information about where to send a subscription order. In response they received 1,000 orders.

I still wasn't particularly impressed. I told them in no uncertain terms what they should have done, which to me was obvious: With the sample newsletter, enclose a letter and *ask for the order,* providing an order card and a reply envelope. They hadn't done any of this.

It's my experience that people almost always ignore free advice, so I really never expected to hear any more.

The Tyndalls had another editorial plug, this time in *Family Circle,* and once again received 10,000 requests for sample copies. This time, they counted 2,000 orders from the sample copies. Lo and behold, they had listened to me and asked for the order. These orders brought their circulation to a total of 6,500.

When they told me about the *Family Circle* results, I finally paid attention and decided there must be more to *Contest News-Letter* than I'd originally thought!

I wrote this letter to the Tyndalls, confirming our

agreement for me to pay them $1,000 for a 49% interest. This was the only contract we ever had. We never had a serious disagreement over the ensuing years.

October 3, 1977
Mr. Richard Benson
5 Water Oak
Amelia Island Plantation
Amelia Island, FL 32034

Mr. Roger Tyndall
P.O. Box 1059
Fernandina Beach, FL 32034

Dear Roger:

As I told you on Saturday, I arrived at 49% because I thought 50/50 was right, but I know that people have hang-ups and I felt you would find it easier to agree to 49%. My own advisers think I am crazy.

As for what I expect to get out of it—my interest is in building a business that will gross $1,000,000 annually and throw off a comparable profit.

Let me restate my proposal:

1) You incorporate - Subchapter S.

2) You go to twelve-time frequency.

3) You go to second-class mail.

4) We have a local accountant keep the books.

5) You go to an outside fulfillment house.

6) Until such time as the new corporation has accumulated enough cash, I will set up a proprietorship to promote new subscriptions. I would do direct-mail promotion at my risk and until such time as I have put at risk a minimum of $25,000. I would have the option to buy for $1,000 a 49% share in the Contest News-Letter.

The new corporation would buy the subscriptions from me on the basis I would eventually receive 110% of my out-of-pocket costs. Since there is no way to foretell the success of these efforts, payment would be made in the following manner so that the ongoing business of the newsletter will not be affected adversely, on the assumption (to be agreed upon) that we can mail newsletters utilizing second-class mail and an outside fulfillment service (for taking care of all the work of addressing customer/complaint/billing reports now done by Carolyn). For $3 per year or a proportionate amount for a shorter period, the balance of monies collected will be paid as collected on account of the promotion. The same will be true for renewals of these promoted subscriptions with an allowance for renewal cost until 110% of the total original promotion cost is paid. For example, let us say in the first promotion of $20,000 we mail 100,000 pieces of mail and generate 5,000 orders at $8. Let us also say 25% does not pay so we collect 3,750 or $30,000. The corporation would retain 3,750 times $3 or $11,250, plus let's say $1 each for the people who do not pay and their attendant costs, for a total then of $12,500. I would receive $17,500 against the $22,000 or 110% of the $20,000 spent. Roughly a year later, if 40% renew, then there will be 1,500 renewals, and if we allow the same $3, plus roughly $1 for renewal promotion, then there would be $6,000 payable to me. Since in this example only $4,500 would be needed to arrive at $22,000, that is all that would be paid.

You should clearly understand, however, that this example provides for promotion at $200 per thousand and that is probably low for the initial test. It also provides for a 5% pull and this is very likely high for the first time out

It is conceivable that it will take three years or more and $100,000 in advances before such a plan was no longer necessary. Unless the first test showed life and a way to be viable we, of course, would not continue.

I don't know what else I can tell you until we try it, except that obviously I believe the whole thing is viable or I wouldn't want to take the gamble.

Sincerely,

Richard V. Benson

P.S. In the additional test we would experiment with $10 as well as $10 for 24 issues of eight pages.

One of my first major moves was to get *Contest News-Letter* tested by Publisher's Clearing House. This test turned out to be a success and we went on to be included by all the stamp-plan companies. We increased the frequency of *Contest News-Letter* to monthly issues and raised the price to $10 a year.

I advanced the money for a mail-order test, which turned out to be a success. As quickly as cash flow permitted, we began making acquisition mailings for subscribers on a regular basis. (Keep in mind we were capitalized for only $2,000.)

The No's from other people's sweepstakes were our best lists, along with active lists of opportunity seekers.

During the last year before we sold *Contest News-Letter,* our total staff consisted of the Tyndalls (who edited the letter), Helen Mullen (my daughter) and myself. Helen and I handled marketing, fulfillment and management. This tiny group was mailing, a million promotion pieces a month to obtain new subscribers and managing the *University of California, Berkeley Wellness Letter,* which we published as a joint venture with Rebus, Inc. (I describe the *Wellness Letter* elsewhere.)

In June, 1986, when we sold *Contest News-Letter* to *McCall's*, the circulation was 750,000 and the business was very profitable. I was ambivalent about selling. My daughter didn't want to sell, but the Tyndalls wanted to bank the money. So I felt that, in the final analysis, it had been their idea and we should sell if that was what they wanted to do.

I THINK *CONTEST NEWS-LETTER* WAS AN OUT-STANDING EXAMPLE OF MY PHILOSOPHY THAT ONE SHOULD DO ONLY THOSE THINGS TO WHICH HE BRINGS A UNIQUE QUALITY. BUY EVERYTHING ELSE AROUND THE CORNER.

Roger Tyndall continued to edit the letter for one year after the sale to *McCall's*. I don't know what Roger and Carolyn plan to do now. They're both still in their forties and certainly don't have to do anything as far as money goes, but my guess is they'll try their talented hands at some new project.

Bob Krefting, who now runs *Contest News-Letter,* has carried my "Make or Buy" thesis to just about the ultimate. He has employed a freelance editor. Even more to his credit, he has employed Rosalie Bruno on a freelance basis to do the day-to-day circulation and production work. Rosalie is a very capable ex-vice president of Knapp Publishing Company as well as former vice president for circulation and development at *Newsweek*. She has now established a business acting as the independent circulation department for several publications.

So Bob Krefting is now the only full-time employee of *Contest News-Letter,* farming out all the functions he doesn't do himself. For *Contest News-Letter* I recently developed a new sweepstakes concept that is in test now; results aren't yet known. In thinking about my next point, bear in mind that *Contest News-Letter* subscribers are avid sweepstakes entrants:

Contest News-Letter has announced and will continually promote that, by random drawing from all the subscribers, the newsletter will each month send out $5,000 in checks with copies of the newsletter. Checks will vary in amount from $2 to $1,000.

On an annual basis, this is a $60,000 cost. With a circulation of 750,000, any measurable impact on pay-up, conversion and/or renewal percentages will produce a profit.

"SOUTHERN LANDMARKS"

"Southern Landmarks" was a series of commemorative porcelain plates, another proprietary business. I joint-ventured this project with Alan Drey, the well known Chicago list-broker.

My first exposure to commemorative plates had been when I worked with Bob Kline of Richmond, VA, marketing a series of plates as a fund-raising project for the Confederate White House Museum. Bob, who now heads the U.S. Historical Society, had an advertising agency, and I had my direct-mail agency, but on this project we were the blind leading the blind. My recollection of this series of plates is 1,201 numbered sets of ten plates, priced at $900 per set. We sold out the numbered sets as well as some 700 unnumbered sets. The museum raised more than $1 million.

I was so taken with this success I decided to enter the commemorative plate business on my own. As a theme, I chose historical houses in the South.

After a successful test, I needed financing for a mass mailing, and I asked Alan Drey to join forces with me. The plates were a limited edition of 10,000 with no designated total number of designs for the series. In other words, it was an "open-end" series.

The plates were manufactured by Gorham, the well-known porcelain company—a fact we made much of. Since we were an unknown company, the use of the Gorham name authenticated the quality of our plates.

We guaranteed the customer the same number with each succeeding plate, which caused a fulfillment and inventory nightmare. If a customer dropped out, we tried to sell a new member as a replacement, but of course we couldn't send him the previous plates he had missed.

We issued roughly two plates a year. In all, we turned out 16 plates which we sold quite profitably.

Incidentally, under New York law, if you issue a limited edition you must either specify the edition limit or (as The Franklin Mint so often did) announce a definite last day for ordering.

IN MERCHANDISING THESE PLATES, WE ONCE AGAIN PROVED THIS RULE OF THUMB: THE SAME MERCHANDISE SOLD AT DIFFERENT PRICES WILL PULL THE SAME TOTAL DOLLARS PER THOUSAND MAILED. WHEN THE INITIAL PLATE WAS SOLD AT $17.50, WE RECEIVED TWICE AS MANY ORDERS AS WHEN IT SOLD AT $35.00. PRICES BETWEEN THE TWO PULLED PROPORTIONATELY.

When we tried to sell plates at $40, the perceived value apparently wasn't there and results fell through the floor.

One problem we experienced was the variety of difficulties encountered in space advertising. We ran successful ads in *Smithsonian* and *Southern Living* magazines. The number of orders, about 500, was insignificant relative to selling 10,000 series starters, even though these orders were economically efficient. Successful tests in those two magazines didn't automatically lead to relatively sure shots in other media, and I felt the price of the chips was just too high to play in large-circulation magazines for the risk involved. I didn't know where to advertise next, and the necessary lead time for space advertising made it impossible to advertise in a large number of magazines, announcing a new product, with any degree of economic safety.

After a few years, inflation caught up with us. Manufacturing costs had gone up drastically, and we were squeezed because we had guaranteed the price per plate to the customer for the life of the series.

Our biggest mistake was in not limiting the guarantee of

price to a predetermined time. It's likely we also made a mistake in promoting the Gorham name, which left us no option of an alternative, less expensive manufacturer as costs increased. We made money, we had fun—but, alas, we had a shorter life span than we might have if we'd taken the proper precautions.

HISTORICAL TIMES PLATES

When Alan Drey and I promoted our "Southern Land-marks" plates, we negotiated for the sponsorship of *American History Illustrated,* one of the magazines published by the Historical Times Company of Harrisburg, PA.

> **OUR EXPERIENCE PROVES ANOTHER RULE OF THUMB: WHENEVER YOU CAN PRESENT A BELIEVABLE REASON FOR A SPECIAL OFFER, RESPONSE WILL BE INCREASED ABOVE AND BEYOND THAT TO BE EXPECTED BY THE DEAL IT-SELF.**

When we sold our plates to the subscribers of *American History Illustrated,* we told them: "Because you are sponsors of the series, you are entitled to buy the plates at $25." This represented a $10 discount from the regular price of $35.

Normally, one could expect a 40% lift for this offer. We actually received more than a 100% lift compared to our orders from a $35 offer to the subscribers of *American History Illustrated's* sister publication, *Early American Life.* The circulation didn't have high duplication, but it would be difficult to differentiate between these two subscriber lists on the basis of demographics or interests.

As a consultant I did a second series of 13 plates based on the original colonies, sponsored by *Early American Life.* We offered the same deal of $10 off to the subscribers of *Early American Life* as sponsors. There, too, we experienced more than a 100% boost instead of the 40% we would normally have expected.

I CAN'T REMEMBER A SINGLE INSTANCE IN
WHICH A SPECIAL DISCOUNT TO CUSTOMERS AS
COMPARED TO OUTSIDERS DIDN'T INCREASE RE-
SPONSE BY MORE THAN THE DISCOUNT.

11

BIG ONES, LITTLE ONES, EASY ONES, TOUGH ONES

HEARST CORPORATION

Hearst Magazines retained me at two different times, spanning several years.

As everyone knows, Hearst is a huge and profitable company. Like Condé Nast, they're superb editorial packagers and great advertising salesmen. They're also very, very good at newsstand sales—aided by their excellent magazine products. The circulation departments of both Hearst and Condé Nast have been newsstand-driven, with subscriptions taking a back seat (a very distant back seat). Direct mail at Hearst is complicated even more by their ownership of a door-to-door sales operation.

For many years, Hearst, had a very weak and backward subscription department; it has been vastly improved since Dick Leventer has been in charge of subscriptions, but the department continues to be subjugated to the rest of the Hearst operations.

When I first worked with Hearst, the company didn't rent or exchange subscription lists; in fact, the rules didn't even allow one Hearst publication to use the subscriber lists of another Hearst magazine, so *Good Housekeeping* couldn't mail to *House Beautiful* subscribers

Hearst didn't use "blow-in" cards, let alone "cross-sell" cards, until Dick Leventer joined them. Even today, by the standards of every publisher I know, Hearst's direct-mail volume is puny. Management's answer to any criticism would be, I feel sure, that they just don't need the additional circulation.

Hearst's low-key direct-mail marketing has allowed the company to be more aggressive than the general industry in pricing subscriptions to their magazines.

To me the key question is whether Hearst magazine circulations are at their optimum levels for total profits. If the answer to that question is yes, then the second question is whether the mix of circulation sources is at the optimum level. During the time I worked for Hearst, I never felt these questions were even addressed, much less answered.

Most of the work we did for Hearst was routine, basic direct marketing. We sold thousands of *Good Housekeeping* subscriptions through the use of freestanding newspaper stuffers.

This was a story in itself: The management at Hearst was unwilling to take the financial risk, so in order to get Hearst to use freestanding stuffers, our agency took the financial risk for its own account and sold the orders to Hearst on a per-order basis.

We made a handsome profit from this arrangement.

PROFESSIONAL FARMERS NEWSLETTER

Professional Farmers is a newsletter published by Merrill Oster in Cedar Falls, Iowa. I worked for Merrill in his early years when his major activity, as a farmer, was finishing pigs.

His newsletter for farmers was essentially a commodity forecasting letter to help farmers market their crops and livestock. The newsletter was expensive, about $68—and that was a number of years ago.

OUR WORK ONCE MORE PROVED THE VALUE OF PREMIUMS AND THAT PREMIUMS DON'T HAVE TO BE RELATED TO THE PRODUCT.

Rather, desirability is the name of the game.

We helped *Professional Farmers* build circulation with attractive offers and merchandise premiums. For the last 15 years calculators and watches have consistently been among the best premiums in direct-mail promotion. We used both.

On one occasion this client said to me, "Benson, you aren't a farmer and you don't understand what appeals to him. We have a new premium that's going to knock the socks off what you've been giving us."

This great idea was a rain gauge.

The next time the group came to see me they brought me a gold-plated rain gauge as well as a long recitation of doggerel on how clients should listen to their consultants. (I wish all clients came to that conclusion.) The reason for all this: They now had a large stock of unwanted rain gauges. The premium had bombed.

Over the following years Merrill Oster, who still is a farmer, has gone on to build a publishing empire of newsletters, *Futures* magazine and seminars. He and Rex Wilmore, his right-hand man, deserve their success. They're intelligent, hard-working, fine gentlemen.

Merrill is a very innovative fellow. To my knowledge, his was the first newsletter to introduce a daily phone tape that his subscribers can call (at the subscriber's expense) to hear Merrill's advice based on that day's market action. Subscriber calls each week amount to some 40% of the subscriber base. What a great idea to enhance involvement—and surely increase renewals.

JOHNSON & JOHNSON

Did you know that Johnson & Johnson, the baby-products company, operates a toy business by mail? J & J has a 10% share of the baby market, an enormous penetration of a market by any mail-order product.

The Johnson & Johnson's product we're discussing is a continuity series of toys geared to the age of the child, beginning soon after birth and shipped automatically every six weeks. My relationship with Johnson & Johnson illustrates a not-uncommon problem: "An idea not invented here (in-house) can't be worth anything."

THE RULE OF THUMB FOR CONTINUITIES IS THAT THE AVERAGE STARTER WILL CONTINUE TO BUY 5 1/2-6 SHIPMENTS.

At the time we worked with them, Johnson & Johnson was having a difficult time. The toys weren't profitable because the company was selling substantially fewer than the normal 5 1/2-6 shipments to each buyer.

Each shipment consisted of two toys priced at $6.95 each. These same toys were also being sold in retail stores. With toys, mail-order selling is particularly difficult, as toys are often the most discounted category of merchandise in retail stores. This makes it tough to provide a rationale for buying by mail.

One of the particularly pertinent problems Johnson & Johnson has is the likelihood of continuing shipments getting out of sync with the child's age due to delays in payment and fulfillment.

The initial Johnson & Johnson offer was this: the first toy free and the second toy for only $4.95 plus shipping. So the basic front-end offer for this series represented an $8 discount. I suggested they sell the toys at full price beginning with the first shipment, and as an incentive offer a premium, with a wholesale cost of $8, for the mother.

My reasoning was that selling at full price might well be a qualifier might make people "stick" longer. I also felt that a premium valued at $15 to $20, which J & J could buy for the same $8 as the discount they were using, might well increase front-end response. We all know how little one panel of a mailing, testing an additional offer, costs.

No test was ever made. Another suggestion I made was to sell a $75-$100 offer at a discount and with a premium, payable in four monthly payments—four payments of $19.95 each. This has three advantages: increasing the average "take," removing the bills and payment from the shipments, and keeping shipments in sync with the child's age. We also proposed several other tests. None of them was tried.

I think there can be little argument that the two tests I've described are testworthy proposals with little downside risk and enormous upside potential. But it became clear to me that no tests were made because the advertising agency and the client felt that any idea not invented by them was not worthwhile.

Unhappily for the consultant, mind-sets and a disposition to distrust ideas from the outside isn't uncommon.

YIELD HOUSE

The Yield House catalog sells Early-American furniture and accent pieces. Yield House also has several retail stores.

Because of inventory problems, Yield House decided to mail a sale catalog in January as a one-time measure. The owners were afraid that, if they did this regularly, customers would wait and buy only from the sale catalog. We convinced management that this wouldn't be the case. The sale catalog became a successful annual feature without detracting from the other Yield House catalogs.

We did extensive testing on shipping and handling charges and found that by including these in the price of the product, instead of showing them as a separate charge, we increased the size of the average order. Our next step was to add a small flat charge ($1) for handling, no matter how many items were in the order. In a poor year that extra $1 charge—which didn't affect response—contributed a major share of profits. Our most successful promotion may have been the addition of a premium for any order. One of our more successful premiums was a wooden peppermill, but the single most successful premium was a mystery gift.

The addition of premiums made it possible for Yield House to successfully mail another catalog in March. This became a major contributor to the dollar gross.

One test proved: It doesn't pay to cut the size of a catalog below the number of pages that will still qualify for a minimum single-piece postage rate. This probably shouldn't have required any proof, but there was much pressure to cut the cost of the catalog in the mail. Not enough attention was being paid to the difference between average costs and incremental costs.

It's self-evident that minimum postage and list costs don't vary with the size of the catalog. The savings in paper and printing costs equal only a small percentage of the total in-the-mail costs.

NATIONAL BELLAS HESS

National Bellas Hess was a chain of discount stores headquartered in Kansas City. For them we developed a series of mailings to increase store traffic and the use of charge accounts.

Prior to a buying season (Easter), we tested doing nothing; we tested a flyer reminding the customer of his credit and the availability of general categories of merchandise; and another test reminding the customer of his credit availability, with an enclosed flyer describing specific merchandise and prices.

Each of these tests showed results better than the previous one. The last test showed that customers bought $8 for each $1 they bought when they weren't circularized.

We continued to mail their charge-account lists at seasonal times with copy about fashion and specific items in the store. Every mailing included an action device. We used a premium to be collected in the store, an upgrade of the customer's charge-account credit limit, sweepstakes that involved a store visit, and even a small limited-time credit balance to the account.

OUR NATIONAL BELLAS HESS EXPERIENCE IS A NEAR-PERFECT EXAMPLE OF THE SUCCESS OF PROMOTIONS BUILT ON BELIEVABLE BENEFITS.

Considering our success in increasing total sales compared to a panel of people to whom the store sent no mailings, I never cease to be surprised at the lack of direct-mail use by the retail world. The fast-food people, grocery chains and gasoline stations have created good mailings. Even for those stores much, much more could be done efficiently. Direct mail is certainly generally missing in any volume from the general retail arena.

WEBB PUBLISHING COMPANY

I brought *Family Handyman* magazine to the attention of the Webb Co. of St. Paul, Minnesota. They bought it for a very low price. structuring the purchase in such a way that they effectively bought the magazine with pretax money.

This is a terrific position to be in. But you have to understand it when you do it.

As you'll see, this story is a wonderful illustration of the importance of making sure that the monthly operating statements serve as management operating tools, not merely as a reflection of the need to pay the IRS. I'm regularly surprised at how often monthly profit-and-loss operating figures don't properly reflect ongoing operations so that they can be used effectively as a management tool.

Let's suppose you buy another company with pretax money. You are quite obviously expensing the purchase price over a period of time. As a result of this, you negatively impact the current operating profits on your profit-and-loss statement.

This is what was happening at *Family Handyman.* Despite great gains in advertising and circulation income, the magazine was losing money every month for several years. *Family Handyman* was the only division of Webb losing money, and it was my impression that management regularly beat up the managers of the magazine.

When I heard complaints about the money they were losing, I kept asking, "What about the present value of the
magazine compared to the initial investment?" The response was, "Present value doesn't show on our books."
From what I was being told, either no one was interested or
no one understood the profits being made from monthly
operations before the purchase price expense.

In my own talks with Webb management, I was sure they
understood what was going on. But it clearly wasn't visible
on the monthly operating statements or in the way they
treated the magazine's managers.

I later had cause to wonder whether the corporate executives themselves really understood what was happening,
when an article appeared in the press indicating that
Handyman was now very profitable. This was after the purchase price had finally been totally expensed. In between,
however, there was a bad morale problem among the managers of the magazine. Regardless, Webb did a fine job of
building a property that was so far down when they bought
it that the previous publisher had stopped mailing renewal
notices. The magazine is now a very valuable property. All
the bad times could have been avoided by a few changes in
monthly operating statements, to reflect a separate cost
item representing the amortization of the purchase price.
This has nothing to do with how a company pays the IRS;
rather, it would mean a clear reflection of monthly operations so that management could have a true picture.

I deplore one practice of the circulation department at
Family Handyman: Reporting to management about renewals, this department always talked about "total renewals"
including both direct to publisher and indirect renewals.

Keep in mind: The contribution of circulation income
was as important as advertising income, or possibly even
more important, relative to the economic health of the
magazine. The largest volume of new subscriptions came
from the stamp plans. These were a positive contribution
even at the low income-per-copy that stamp plans remit.

But the real impact on per-copy income came from direct-
to-publisher renewals. Indirect renewals, primarily renewals received from stamp plans, had almost no positive

impact and were certainly no more valuable than new business from the stamp plans.

By incorporating indirect renewals in their renewal reports, the circulation department looked better because the percentage number was higher. But I always felt they were misleading an unsophisticated management.

One of Webb's other consumer magazines was *Snow Goer*, a magazine for snowmobile owners. Circulation was obtained by promoting the names of snowmobile owners obtained from warranty cards. For this magazine we developed a very successful sweepstakes—a drawing, not a lucky-number sweeps.

Contest News-Letter reported this sweepstakes in one of its issues. The result was that the grand prize of two snowmobiles was won by a subscriber of *Contest News-Letter*—who lived in Florida.

12
FRIENDLY ONES, CONTROVERSIAL ONES, SNOOTY ONES, EDIBLE ONES

RESPONSE DEVELOPMENT CORPORATION

Response Development Corporation was a direct-mail agency operated by John Swain and specializing in, but not limited to, fund raising. John was an old friend whom I had known since his early days in the magazine agency world.

I consulted with John for several years, mostly about routine fundamentals. Two innovations I brought him, which he didn't test until several years after I was no longer consulting for him, resulted in the mailing of millions of successful mailing pieces.

I originated the idea of inducing donations from donors on the house donor list to establish a "Challenge Fund." The appeal to house-list donors would be that their donations would go twice as far because we'd use the money to generate matching funds from a new group of donors.

It's obvious: When you ask someone to donate to your cause, you enhance the appeal tremendously when you can say you're establishing a matching fund to be used to generate a like amount from new donors—so in effect his donation will go twice as far. The converse of this is that when you approach a new donor, you can talk about the matching fund, which will match his donation and make *his* money go twice as far.

The goal of all direct mail is to cause the recipient to take some action. We use sweepstakes to reward the recipient by giving him a chance to win a large reward. We often use premiums to induce the reader to buy or even to take advantage of a free trial. Copy that pushes for a Yes or No answer is another such device.

Imagine, if you will, the power of a live check made out to a charity by the matching fund, as an enclosure in a mailing to a new potential donor. The recipient now has the problem of doing something with a real check. Does his conscience allow him to throw it away? Does he return it with no donation? Does he send it back with a donation?

When John finally used the matching-check concept, it was one of the best promotion devices he ever employed. He was the first fund raiser to take advantage of this concept.

All these devices—sweepstakes, premiums, Yes or No copy and live checks—are designed to force a decision to action. As promoters, we know that if we can get prospects to make a decision rather than do nothing, we'll get more people to take positive action.

I believe John Swain was the first to use sweepstakes in fund raising. This was an innovation that I had repeatedly urged him to try several years before he did it for the first time.

The secret ingredient for a successful fund-raising sweepstakes is to have the prizes donated so that none of the cause's money is used for such frivolity.

RICHARD VIGUERIE

Richard Viguerie is "Mr. Conservative" and has been the principal fund raiser for political candidates representing the right wing of the Republican party. He is also a major fund-raiser for various charities.

Richard is a fine gentleman who totally believes in the program of the Right, so much so that he regularly risks the very viability of his company on his political beliefs. One must admire him no matter what one's politics are, because he truly stands up and is counted for what he believes. All of us suffer from the fact that too few people are willing to do this.

Richard Viguerie is a master of involvement. He has a rule cast in concrete for his copywriters: Every mailing will make use of an involvement device.

Although I don't remember the specifics, I sometimes thought the involvement was reaching too far or even got in the way of the mailing's purpose, but overall I believe it is a useful rule. Involvement does work, and I suppose the way to be sure it isn't overlooked is to make it an ironclad rule without exceptions.

One of Viguerie's favorite involvement devices was the survey. Another was preprinted postcards to your congressmen.

Before I joined Viguerie he frequently used membership as a device, but for some reason didn't follow up for the next year's dues. I don't mean his organization didn't follow up their donors (members). They did, and regularly; but the follow-ups didn't include membership dues for the following year.

At my suggestion, they began to follow up members the next year in an organized fashion, with a billing series for the new year's dues. Even though the dues were generally low, the percentage of payers was so high it quickly became one of the best annual fund-raising efforts for several of his accounts. This was no more than applying the practices of the profit-making marketing practitioners to fund raising.

BY THE WAY: IN MY EXPERIENCE, MEMBERSHIP RENEWAL IS REGULARLY TEN POINTS ABOVE SUBSCRIPTION LEVELS. THIS IS THE RESULT OF BILLING FOR DUES RATHER THAN ASKING FOR A RENEWAL OF MEMBERSHIP.

Another innovation I brought to Viguerie was the matching-check program (described under Response Development Corporation).

Richard successfully added his own twist to the matching-check idea when he used multiple checks with different dates to the same donor. He substantially increased the total funds raised in political campaigns by using three checks to be sent on a one-a-month basis. What he really did was institute installment payments—without calling them that.

SMITHSONIAN

I was retained by *Smithsonian* to help launch their magazine. Happily, I'm still associated with them some 18 years later.

Smithsonian was a great circulation success from the very first test mailing. Their success stems from having a very fine editorial product and good promoters; but contributing to their success even more than the promoters is the power of the Smithsonian name. I know of no other instance of a name being so important. The closest similarity is the value to *Southern Living* that Southerners are Southerners are Southerners.

One of the interesting facts about *Smithsonian* is that the demographics of *Smithsonian* subscribers, who had very high income when the circulation was 200,000, have kept pace with the tremendous growth of the magazine, even after allowing for inflation. The demographics of their members are relatively the same now that circulation is more than 2 million. This just proves that a magazine pulls its own audience.

During the years when *Smithsonian* was growing from 200,000 to 2 million, it was easily one of the very largest mailers in the country (as many as 40-50 million pieces). Despite such large-quantity mailings, the subscriber demographics weren't diluted.

When the Smithsonian built the new Asia Museum, we were asked to help raise a substantial amount of money from the Smithsonian Associates (subscribers). Once again I proved that it was better to ask for a specific gift ($35) than to use the normal fund-raising approach of multiple suggested amounts ($500, $200, $100, $25 or "other"). The single suggested figure of $35 was a higher average gift than the multiple-suggestion offer, and substantially more people responded at the single figure of $35.

KNAPP PUBLISHING

One of the successful innovations we introduced at Knapp (the publisher of *Architectural Digest, Home* and *Bon Appétit* magazines) was the "fancy label." The fancy label was the invention of Leo Yochim, president of Printronics in New York. He put a colored border on a cheshire label and, for whatever reason, it increased response.

I had worked for *Bon Appétit* when Pillsbury owned it. At Pillsbury it was a bimonthly and wasn't doing very much. I went to Bud Knapp and suggested he could buy it for "a dollar and a due bill." He did buy it (not for a dollar but for not much more). It has been reported in the trade press that the price was $60,000. Bud turned *Bon Appétit* into an important and successful monthly magazine.

Architectural Digest was one of many magazines that found success with fancy labels.

This story about the book division of Knapp illustrates the consequences of bad testing:

The division had conducted a seasonality test by mailing segments of the same lists every month to measure the effect or response of the season. The results showed very little deviation by month. The book division tested a new cookbook in late December, with good results. Based on their seasonality study, they rolled out in May—with disastrous results. It really wasn't surprising since May is a poor mailing month for most products.

When I looked into "Why the disaster?" I found the seasonality test had been done with 30-day hotline names.

THIRTY-DAY HOTLINE NAMES WILL OVERCOME SEASONALITY. THAT WAS THE REASON THAT THIS SEASONALITY TEST SHOWED VERY LITTLE DIFFERENCE IN MONTH-BY-MONTH RESULTS.

The basic fact is: December, when they tested, is a good mailing season. May isn't.

WARNING! If you think you've discovered a window of opportunity (in terms of mailing) in what is generally considered an off month or season, proceed with caution.

GOODBEE PECAN

Goodbee Pecan is a unique story more for the *raison d'être* of its mail-order business than for any innovation of mail marketing. The company is a pecan marketing co-op in Albany, Georgia, the original home of pecan groves in the United States. The operator-owners are the Weatherbee family, a wealthy and prominent Albany family.

When Mike, the youngest family member, came into the business he was given the assignment of learning as much as possible about direct marketing. Keep in mind that Albany, Georgia, is rural country, hardly the center of the universe or a fountainhead of marketing.

The impetus for the decision to have Mike learn direct marketing was this: So many pecan groves were being planted in the Southwest that the total United States pecan crop would grow by 40%. There were no grounds to believe that there would be a corresponding growth in demand. The co-op was seeking a meaningful new way to market pecans directly to the consumer.

With the help of their previous consultant, they had

attempted to sell pecans as business gifts. Many of us have received, as a Christmas business gift, pecans beautifully hand-packed in a plastic container. But I have never been successful in directly approaching the business-gift market.

It's particularly difficult with food as a product because the necessary price discounts aren't available. Business-gift donors want to use an item that looks like $20 and costs $10. You just can't do that with food and have a perceived value at the stated full price.

When I joined Goodbee, I changed their strategy. We went after the general public. We extended the line to include not only raw pecans, but salted and in-shell nuts and pecan candy in various size packs. Remember our primary brief: to move tonnage of pecans.

We developed a 16-page, four-color catalog with a bound-in order form that we mailed in an envelope with a separate letter and an additional separate order form and reply envelope. For several years we were quite successful, but in recent years new-buyer acquisition has been too expensive. Repeat business continues to be excellent.

Unlike most food items, there really is no "super grade" pecan, so it's impossible to deliver a unique or better product except when you make candy. In candy, I don't think Goodbee did a particularly super job of producing a unique or better product.

Let me tell you how pecans are picked, shelled and graded, so you can understand the lack of a super grade for use in direct mail.

At harvest time, workers attach a belt like a reducing machine to the tree and shake it. Then the nuts, twigs and whatever else falls down is vacuumed up from the ground and placed in 10,000-pound trailers. The trailer-load becomes the control unit for ultimate payment to the grove owner.

The trailer is then placed in a field and a hairdryer-like device is attached to dry the whole thing out. The trailer is then taken to the sheller, a two-story Rube Goldberg-type machine. When the trailer is unloaded into the machine, it sorts the nuts into three sizes; using wire brushes against

SECRETS OF SUCCESSFUL DIRECT MAIL

a steel plate, the outer shell is removed. Then it's back to the trailers, to the field, and to another session with the dryer.

Now we go back to the sheller, where a conveyor belt carries the nuts up two floors to be cracked one at a time. Most of the shell falls off and the nuts are floated across some water, where the rest of the shell falls off.

Then the nuts pass under an ultraviolet light which grades them by color. At the end of the belt, they're jiggled (like panning for gold) and the pieces are separated from the halves by hand.

There are some 38 grades, but 65% are the number-one grade. In fact, perfect halves have to be broken for the commercial trade.

Goodbee moved into the fund-raising arena, which has turned out to be a very successful area. As the result of all this specialized retail marketing, the co-op has been able to return to the growers a substantial premium over the wholesale price.

Mike Weatherbee learned his lessons well. My hat is off to Goodbee for what I think is the most forward-thinking program I have known. And imagine, out of rural Georgia.

CREST FRUIT

Crest Fruit markets Ruby Red grapefruit from Texas under the name Frank Lewis. When I first joined the company, Frank Schultz and Fred Petch were the principals. Frank is a very aggressive and innovative direct mail marketer, a talented copywriter and a fine gentleman. Even better, he's a willing promotion-tester.

Frank has the Puritan work ethic and a drive to work hard 12 months a year. Most people would love to have a good business that operates eight months, like the mail-order grapefruit business, but Frank was determined to extend the business year-round.

Fred was in charge of production and thought of himself as being in the grapefruit business. He had no trouble with an eight-month business, vacationing the rest of the year. I have a tremendous admiration for Fred and for his love of life. After reaching the age of 60, Fred has lived more than most people do in a lifetime. He took up hang-gliding; he qualified for a pilot's license; and he has a large boat that he uses frequently. He lives life to the fullest.

Crest purchased the grapefruit crop from the grove owners while it was still on the trees and used their own fruit pickers for harvesting. This allowed Crest to stretch out the season and pick fruit according to their needs. (Citrus, unlike other types of fruit, can stay on the trees for months after ripening without spoiling and falling to the ground.)

One result of operating this way and buying the total crop is the problems that arose from the enormous tonnage of commercial fruit that has to be disposed of to the wholesale trade. The commercial sale resulted in large annual losses.

Only a small part (perhaps 5%) of the crop—fruit that was extra-large and unblemished—was suitable for sale by mail under the Frank Lewis name. Crest sells grapefruit utilizing a club format with automatic shipping of fruit to the members every few weeks.

Crest also had a Christmas catalog selling grapefruit in various packages and in combination with other products such as avocados, oranges and pineapples. They also sold goods they bought for resale, such as dried fruit and fruitcake. Those latter items, when inventory losses were considered, produced little or no profit.

In the summer Crest used its work force to personalize paper napkins, which they sold to their house list of grapefruit buyers. This was all in pursuit of Frank's desire to work all year.

I helped push Crest out of the napkin business and out of selling many of the items they bought from other suppliers and didn't produce themselves. They also reduced their dependence on buying the crop on the trees and are now buying a substantial amount of premium fruit only, instead of all grades, from the local co-op. All this has had a beneficial effect on Crest profits and has reduced the tonnage of commercial fruit with its consequent losses.

Crest had to decide: Are you primarily in the grapefruit business or in the direct-mail marketing business?

THIS IS ANOTHER ILLUSTRATION OF THE BENEFIT OF CLOSELY EXAMINING THE "MAKE OR BUY" QUESTION.

13

THE

POLK

CONNECTION

The R. L. Polk Co., in addition to being one of the largest list compilers in the country, operates a major direct-mail agency.

Fred Zimmermann, vice president and national marketing manager of Polk, virtually created this division. He formed it, nurtured it and raised it to its present size. Judging by number of pieces mailed, I venture to say Polk is one of the largest direct-mail agencies in the country, if not the largest.

In my many years of working with Polk, I was involved in solving direct-mail problems for many of their clients. For example:

EXXON

Exxon marketed travel-club memberships to its credit-card holders. The club was unique in that it was built around the primary benefit of accidental-death insurance ($20,000 for the member and $10,000 for the spouse).

This is a common policy in the insurance business, but I don't believe any insurance company has ever successfully sold it through the mail. Exxon added a major twist: If husband and wife were both killed in the same accident, the policy paid $100,000. This enhancement turned a mediocre offer into a great offer.

Additional club benefits included travel guides, trip routing, *Vista* magazine and bail bond.

Exxon had one tremendous additional competitive advantage: They were able to bill the customer on his monthly gasoline bill. This has two implicit benefits: (1) reducing the amount of each payment; and (2) taking advantage of inertia. The amount charged each month is small and the customer tends to ignore it.

Even if he decides to cancel, he procrastinates, delaying implementation of the decision. Canceling is too much trouble. The membership life of a travel-club member is substantially longer than the renewal life of a parallel policyholder of a conventional insurance company.

The monthly charges ranged from $2.75 to $3.50. Membership reached a level of one million.

THIS ILLUSTRATES A FINE RULE OF THUMB: ANY TIME YOU CAN BILL TO A CREDIT CARD OR CHARGE ACCOUNT FOR A CONTINUITY PRODUCT, THE LONGEVITY OF THE CUSTOMER OR TOTAL "TAKE" WILL BE GREATLY INCREASED.

The travel club was also promoted to people who weren't Exxon credit-card holders. They were given the option of paying their dues quarterly through their Visa or MasterCard. The results weren't as good as monthly billing on the Exxon credit card, but they were still very successful, much more so than selling on an annual "bill me" mode.

We made a major breakthrough in our promotions when, at my behest, Exxon made an offer of the first two months for $1. This increased acceptance and maximized the use of monthly billing on the credit card with its inherent inertia factor.

One of our most successful offers, which continued for a number of years, was using a garment bag as a premium.

This is one of the best examples I've seen of the success of premiums that are desirable and have perceived value. It could be said that this premium was related to the product, but that was secondary to its success. A garment bag has high perceived value, and this appeals to greed.

Exxon tested many premiums over the years, including more expensive items offered at a self-liquidating cost. A self-liquidating premium seemed like a great idea, but it was a bomb. I think the reason for this is that when you ask for even a partial payment for a premium, you're left in the position of selling two things—your product and the premium—at once. This is a primary "no-no" of direct mail.

We did get a substantial lift on results when we used two premiums. In addition to the garment bag we offered a pickpocket-proof wallet, which had proved to be a good premium when used by itself.

The president of the travel club, Bill Rowland, loved nothing better than adding benefits for the members. Management's orders were that promotion copy had to spell out each and every one of the benefits.

The trouble with this is that while all direct-mail copy is hard sell, there's no way to sell 21 benefits without screaming at the top of your lungs.

When finally, after years had gone by, we were allowed to develop a new-member promotion concentrating on our four major benefits and only listing the others, results improved. This is a fine illustration of the need for copy to be interesting; and while we all know (or should know) that copy is "benefits, benefits, benefits," there's no way to stay as interesting as we should while talking about 21 separate benefits.

For a number of years, I had urged Exxon to raise prices, particularly when they would "cry poor," or when acquisition costs increased; but my pleas fell on deaf ears.

THE TRAVEL CLUB IS AN EXAMPLE OF ONE OF THE MOST COMMON SHORTCOMINGS IN OUR INDUSTRY, PARTICULARLY IN PUBLISHING. IF WE ASSUME PROFIT IS THE BASIC MOTIVE OF BUSINESS (EXXON MIGHT ARGUE THIS ASSUMPTION),

THEN, LIKE SO MANY OTHER COMPANIES, EXXON DID A POOR JOB OF PROBING PRICES. I DON'T BELIEVE A TEST OF HIGHER PRICES WAS EVER MADE.

Maximum profit results from the right balance of price, cost of selling and lifetime purchases. At Exxon we never found out the effect of a price increase. Can you imagine the effect on profits of an increase of $.25 per month to a million members? The company could afford to lose a large number of members and still be ahead.

TRAVELER'S INSURANCE COMPANY

Traveler's offer of insurance by mail improved dramatically when we added steak knives as a premium.

THIS IS ANOTHER EXAMPLE OF PREMIUM DESIRABILITY, NOT PRODUCT RELATIONSHIP.

HARVARD MEDICAL LETTER

In addition to its activities as a direct-mail agency, Polk has also been involved in a number of newsletters as joint ventures. The *Harvard Medical Letter* is the most outstanding example. With Polk's expertise it became the largest newsletter of its type.

One of the strangest characteristics of the *Harvard Medical Letter* promotion is the control package. It is and has been in a 9"×12" format. Imagine a mailing selling a newsletter—no pictures, no color—with a 9"×12" control promotion package. (Time-Life Books, Grolier, Meredith and Field Publications all successfully use the 9"×12" format, but the fact remains that the 9"×12" size represents only a small percentage of total direct mail.) Polk has tested different formats but hasn't been able to beat the Harvard 9"×12" control mailing.

This proves so well: You never can make 100% rules

about promotion. You'll almost always find an exception to any rule.

Harvard took advantage of its list of subscribers by publishing and selling a health-oriented cookbook. The successful offer sold the book for three installment payments. The use of installment payments increased orders by 25%.

> MY RULE OF THUMB FOR THE INCREASE OF ORDERS GENERATED BY THE USE OF INSTALLMENT PAYMENTS IS 15%.

HARVARD MENTAL HEALTH LETTER

Profits of the *Harvard Mental Health Letter* were substantially increased by an offer I suggested. It combined the magic of "FREE" with the value of quarterly billing to a bank credit card.

The offer was this: Three months free, then quarterly billing of $9.75. Polk estimates that, by the end of three years, increased profits will be $7.35 (19%) for each starting subscription. With this offer the *Mental Health Letter* experienced an increase of 25% in paid starters.

Even more important, Polk anticipates that after three years the *Letter* will have 125% more continuing subscribers on the credit card offer than on the straight subscription. The long-term increase in profits is enormous.

> THIS ILLUSTRATES THE POSITIVE EFFECT OF OPEN-END BILLING TO A CREDIT CARD. THERE'S NO EXPIRATION AND THEREFORE NO RENEWAL DECISION.

There is a credit-card cost but no other collection expenses and no renewal expenses and no bad pay with this offer.

FORBES

Polk some years ago introduced Yes-No-Maybe stickers on the order card of their promotion mailings. With this device they were selling a soft offer (take a complimentary —FREE—copy and if you don't like it write "cancel" on the bill). In the original versions the Yes and Maybe contracts were for the same term.

I proposed the idea that Yes should be a long-term offer and Maybe a short-term offer. This version became the winner at Forbes.

BANTAM BOOKS

Bantam Books was another Polk client.

Years ago I was struck by the lack of credibility of a ten-day or 14-day examination offer. The publisher or mailer doesn't truly mean it because he accepts returns at virtually any point.

On the other hand, the prospect may be turned off doubts about when the FREE examination period actually starts. Is it when the product is shipped? The seller might perceive the time is up just when he receives the item.

We tested and conclusively proved there was a pronounced increase in orders when copy specified 21 days free examination instead of a shorter period.

I had not made this test in some years but once again it proved successful when Polk tested the 21-day examination versus the old control of ten days at Bantam.

AMOCO

Amoco has a major motor club, which the oil company sells to its credit-card holders. This is a traditional stop-and-go club: Like AAA, Amoco will respond when you have auto trouble.

Unlike Exxon, over the years Amoco has aggressively probed higher prices and in fact has raised prices more than once. Profits increased, but, as was to be expected, returns from acquisition mailings were reduced.

Amoco charged the annual club fee in a single billing on the gasoline credit card. For several years I urged the company at least to break the charge into three or four installments, but they resisted because for one reason or another they couldn't handle it at their credit-card center.

Finally we did convince them to make a test and handle the back end by hand if they couldn't program it into the computers. Order results were very much improved but it was still a very long time (my recollection: two to three years) before they could implement installment payments at their computer center. They have now gone to quarterly billing, which is even better than installments. If they would go to monthly billing, they would have even better results.

THE OFFER OF INSTALLMENT PAYMENTS IN-CREASES ORDERS.

There's no doubt in my mind that Amoco has lost millions and millions of dollars in profits because they haven't been willing to force their credit centers to handle monthly installment payments. We know the positive effect on acquisition costs when monthly billing is implemented, and the inertia factor of no renewal decision has a positive-increase effect on membership longevity.

Overall, Amoco has done a superb job of offsetting credit-card costs by selling enhanced cards and services to their cardholders. I venture to say they've done this far better than any other major oil company.

SUNSET MAGAZINE

Sunset is a very successful magazine, published in California. It was the first regional (several states) magazine.

Sunset and the *New Yorker* are, I believe, are the only two major magazines sold primarily by subscription that don't offer subscribers the "bill me" option.

Several years ago, through Polk, I urged *Sunset* to test credit. The results of a credit offer were a 20% improvement (my rule of thumb is a 50-100% improvement) in the cost of orders.

Sunset didn't implement the use of credit, and as far as I know still hasn't implemented it.

Some time after the credit test, I was involved in a telephone conference call. The *Sunset* people were looking for some new "breakthrough" idea for circulation acquisition mailings. When I asked why *Sunset* didn't implement the credit option I was told they felt they didn't need it. I confess I didn't understand this answer.

BRANIGAR

Branigar is a real estate development company owned by Union Camp. Polk had developed a mailing package for Branigar, promoting The Landings at Skidaway Island, a residential development in Georgia. After several years of mailings Polk was about to lose the client.

Polk sent the mailing package to me for a critique. I could find nothing wrong and I couldn't find any constructive additions to make. Since I lived at Amelia Island, FL, only a little more than 100 miles south of Skidaway Island, I drove up to look at The Landings.

The results were that I bought a lot, built a house and moved, and we love living at The Landings. Sad to say, Polk lost the account, but I believe Branigar is still using the same promotion piece.

ETHICS OF A REAL ESTATE DEVELOPER

I don't remember the name of their client, but Polk invited me to participate in a sales presentation to a real-estate developer in Washington, D.C.

This was at a time when there were 54 developers of second homes whose sites were within 90 minutes of Washington. They all were dialing numbers from the phone book each week, trying to get prospects to visit their particular properties.

Let me lay a little groundwork: When I first came into the magazine business I was told of all the evils of door-to-door magazine salesmen. I was given to believe they were the hardest sales people around, not to be admired. In fact,

I often teased Lester Suhler, a vice president of *Look* magazine, that while *Look* didn't pay very well, they did let him make a lot of money supplying fake prosthetic devices to their door-to-door sales force.

After I became acquainted with the encyclopedia business I decided that magazine salesmen were pantywaists. Encyclopedia salesmen were taught to get in the door and spread their books around. Then, using a script that included three false closings (a false closing refers to the moment when you think the salesman is finally going to tell you the price and he gets right up to it and then backs away without telling you), they built to the inevitable pressure-laden close.

Our presentation went on with Polk telling the prospects how much we knew about direct mail and the real estate people telling us about selling land. Their stories of the methods used in selling land made encyclopedia salesmen seem pure as the driven snow.

The meeting had gone on for some time and it was clear we weren't going to make a sale. One of the real estate people finally turned to us and said, "Let's cut out the small talk. What we need is something big. For instance, if you could put a 'Detour' sign up on the highway so people were forced to come by the property we'd sell one out of three of them."

Now there is a creative solution to a marketing problem. What's more, I'll bet they would have sold one out of three people if we'd been able to put up the "Detour" sign.

FINGERHUT

On another occasion Polk invited me to be part of a presentation selling Polk's compiled list to Fingerhut.

At the time, Fingerhut and New Process were two of the most prominent mail-order companies in the country. Each was doing a business of $200 million or more through direct mail. Fingerhut used mail-order lists and New Process mailed compiled lists.

The meeting of about a dozen people had already started when I arrived. Julian Haydon, who was Polk's general manager, had told the group, "Benson is coming. He won't say much but you should damn well listen to him."

Julian was always somewhat nervous when I attended Polk-client meetings because I was as apt to be a Polk adversary as an advocate. Actually, on balance this worked to Polk's advantage because it was always clear that I was independent, and it was to their credit to bring in an independent outside consultant.

As can happen in meetings of this size, the session dragged on for a couple of hours without any real progress. It was finally my turn and I spoke perhaps 50 words about what was obvious: "If another company as large as New Process was extensively using compiled lists and I weren't, I'd have to test to see what they knew that I didn't."

That pretty well ended the meeting. Fingerhut did test the Polk list.

SALK NEWSLETTER

At one point Polk discussed with me the advisability of doing a newsletter with Lee Salk, the famous child psychologist. I advised against it for two reasons: my negative experience with another parenting newsletter, and the enormous problems I had encountered when I dealt with products concerning preschool children on behalf of another client.

Polk ignored my advice and went ahead with a test mailing. The initial results exceeded their expectations. The Polk people then planned a trip to see me in Georgia, with the test results in hand. They were gleeful because they felt they had me on the defensive: "For the first time in his history with us Benson was wrong." My track record with Polk had been so good that they were happy to catch me in the wrong about a new product.

Before the Polk people had their meeting with me, early pay-up figures became available. They showed that with 10% pay-up, Salk had 40% cancellation. No second mailing was made and my record at Polk remained unblemished.

14

A
SHORT CHAPTER:
WHAT I'M
DOING NOW

THE *UNIVERSITY OF CALIFORNIA, BERKELEY WELLNESS LETTER*

The name is a mouthful, but necessary. I'm told there are more than 160 health-oriented newsletters.

I got the idea for the *Wellness Letter* in 1983, with the advent of Owen Lipstein's *American Health* magazine, which was an immediate circulation success.

I had worked on the *Harvard Medical Letter* as well as the *Tufts Nutrition Letter,* both of which were published by the R. L. Polk Co.; but I was taken with *American Health's* positive editorial outlook, contrasted with the disease orientation of so many health letters.

I conceived a newsletter rather than a magazine for two primary reasons: (1) I felt that in the perception of many people, the editorial authenticity of a magazine would be tainted by advertising; (2) I knew little or nothing about the sale of advertising.

Searching for a source of editorial material, I found Rodney Friedman, president of Rebus, Inc., an editorial packaging house. Among the accomplishments of Rebus is a continuity series about cooking for Time-Life Books. Two more continuity series of books for Time-Life are in the works. Rodney's reputation for quality is unmatched.

Instead of having Rodney become my supplier, we decided to form a joint venture between his company and Tyndall Publishing. I had one caveat: I didn't want to publish unless we could get a medical school as a sponsor to provide authenticity.

It took us a year of searching before we came to an agreement with the University of California, Berkeley. (Berkeley is the number-one public health school in the country.)

The *Wellness Letter* is an eight-page monthly with an annual subscription price of $20.00.

We've been very aggressive promoters and are sold almost 100% by direct mail. We currently mail at an annual level of 15 million pieces. We're able to mail at such a high volume because we work at finding lists and take advantage of segmenting our lists based on zip penetration.

Incidentally, the marketing and management staff still consists only of my daughter and myself. Editorial work is done by Rebus. The content is then vetted and approved by the faculty of the University of California, Berkeley.

In less than three years, *Wellness* has reached a level of 500,000 subscriptions. We're the number-one health letter in terms of circulation. None of our three largest competitors has a circulation of even 300,000 subscribers.

When I conceived the *Wellness Letter,* I felt that reaching 250,000 circulation and breaking even on a profit-and-loss basis would be a success, because we'd be doing something good and making an important contribution. To say I'm proud of our success and our product, which my partner Rodney Friedman puts together so expertly, is to put it mildly.

As you can see once again, I practice what I preach about my "Make or Buy" philosophy.

15

SOME
DEFINITIONS—
AND
SOME OPINIONS

Note: Some campaigns fail just because those who originate them ignore or misinterpret results. Creativity is only half the game; analysis is the other half. Have you paid attention to:

BOGIES

A bogey is the maximum allowable cost of acquisition of a new buyer.

Calculating the maximum allowable cost for acquiring a new customer is simple. It's also the only way to maximize the amount of your promotion mail and, in turn, maximize your profits.

The following method is useful for continuities, memberships, subscriptions, catalogs or any program with the potential of a second sale:

The lifetime value of each first-time customer is ultimately the answer to profits. In most instances, if you break even on a cumulative basis with the second sale, there will be no question of eventual satisfactory profits.

This is a much more liberal policy than most companies practice. Yes, there are some instances in which waiting until the third sale to break even is practical. But the major problem with going beyond the second sale is the question of how many more sales will be made to the average customer, as well as the question of the time element and how long you can finance the customer at a loss.

I'll illustrate, using actual calculations for my *Wellness Letter*.

In this example the newsletter costs $4 a year to fulfill. Bad pay is $.50 on a renewal subscription. Conversion-promotion costs are $.75 per expire. With a conversion percentage of 33%, the promotion cost of each renewal becomes $2.25.

The total costs for promoting and fulfilling a conversion subscription are $6.75. Income is $20. Therefore contribution from a conversion for each starter subscription is $13.25 divided by three, or $4.42.

Acquisition promotion mail costs $240 per thousand.

Newsletter costs of fulfillment are $4.

Bad pay is $1 for a new subscription.

The introductory price is $15.

Income of $15 less $5 cost of fulfillment leaves $10. If we add the $4.42 second-year contribution to the $10 first-year contribution we have $14.42 before acquisition costs.

Direct-mail costs are $240 per thousand. At a $14.42 acquisition cost we need a 1.66% net order response to break even on the second sale.

On the basis of these numbers we should acquire every possible order where the last order acquired costs no more than $14.42, or 1.66%, from mailings.

Note very carefully: This is not the average for the mailing but rather the return percentage for the last list used in the promotion mailing. The overall average return percentage should be substantially higher, if this 1.66% is the return from the bottom list we use.

In our example we don't want to go below 1.66% because we're saying that below that we never experience an acceptable profit. We know there will always be some surprises, but the formula has enough cushion to withstand almost any shock.

In addition, consider: We haven't included list rental income. In this case list rental would add another $1.50 for the first sale and add $.50 to the contribution for the second sale. If this $2 is added to the allowable cost of $14.42 we get $16.42, or a needed percentage of only 1.46%.

An acceptable return percentage of 1.46% instead of 1.68% could well increase the potential list universe by as much as 30-50%. The fact is, we're actually using a loose 1.8% bogey for our newsletter and presently mailing at an annual level of 15 million.

We are three years old and we started with a limited amount of capital. As we gain more experience I believe we can reach an annual promotion mailing level of as much as 30 million.

Don't dismiss that 30 million figure. Yes, it's substantially more promotion than most companies mail. It isn't just due to our specific product, a newsletter on health. Consider our three biggest competitors, the Harvard, Mayo, and Tufts newsletters. Each mails no more than 5 million (my guess) a year. The answer, I believe, lies in the use of a proper bogey, plus (as I have said many times) the lack of work in the list area by most mailers.

Contrast the above analysis with what goes on in too many companies. Budgeting is most often done on the basis of historical trends rather than calculation of the maximum allowable cost for acquisition of an order.

Catalogs generally seek to break even on cold mail. How much more aggressive they could be using the above formula! Magazines frequently have a formula for acquiring subscriptions on the basis of trading promotion dollars for circulation dollars the first year and incurring the cost of fulfillment. Of course I'm primarily talking about magazines that are circulation-driven, not advertising-driven.

There's no great difficulty adjusting the bogey to accommodate magazines with advertising revenue. I haven't lost sight of the fact that this formula has a capital requirement, but that doesn't alter another fact: it's a viable formula and a proper business decision.

TESTING

Testing can almost be described as the be-all and end-all of direct-mail marketing. Testing can and should play a major part in deciding whether a new product might be viable.

Concept testing was, I believe, first done by *Reader's Digest.* Concept testing is a survey of potential buyers, outlining a number of possible products and asking the reader to choose the one of four possible answers that best reflects his likelihood to buy or not to buy.

Several of my clients have used this technique. Its success has led me to the conclusion that concept testing should be mandatory whenever a new product is contemplated. It's my opinion that a given concept test should be limited to six products, two of which should represent past products as controls or benchmarks; one of these should be a winner and the other a loser. Trying to test more products runs the risk of reader boredom and false results.

I believe the price point should also be stated in the description of each product.

After a successful concept test, the next step is a dry test. A dry test is one in which you haven't yet made the decision to go into business with this particular product. It's particularly suitable where the product still has to be developed.

Copy may or may not expressly state that you haven't made up your mind (see the section on *U.S. News*) or may refer to the product as "when published" or "when available." Only credit orders may be solicited since you won't be able to ship within 30 days. If you specify a date for shipment, then you can solicit and accept cash; but I'm assuming this is a true dry test: You haven't yet made up your mind to be in this particular business. It's my policy that a proper dry test requires a 150,000-piece mailing. Such a mailing would be a variation of this grid:

| Lists | Package A | | | Package B | Package C |
	Offer 1	Offer 2	Offer 3	Offer 1	Offer 1
1	3,000	3,000	3,000	3,000	3,000
2	3,000	3,000	3,000	3,000	3,000
3	3,000	3,000	3,000	3,000	3,000
4	3,000	3,000	3,000	3,000	3,000
5	3,000	3,000	3,000	3,000	3,000
6	3,000	3,000	3,000	3,000	3,000
7-18	(5000 each) 60,000				
	78,000	18,000	18,000	18,000	18,000

Based on this breakout, you can see I've tested three copy packages, three offers and 18 lists. The results should give a good answer for the best copy, the right offer and the potential universe. I've never had any trouble combining the response of Offers 2 or 3 with Copy B or C, should one of these combinations be the winner, rather than A.

Note: The first six lists should have large potential universes.

I know many people will test in smaller quantities, but it's my feeling that you should strive for a black or white answer, not a gray one, which would require retesting. If possible, I want to answer all "what if" questions in the first test. Life is too short to keep retesting in order to answer the "what ifs" before making a product decision.

I also want enough answers so that I can roll out a substantial mailing to launch my new product.

There's never enough money to test every element of a mailing or everything one would like to test. In my opinion, it's more important to test packages than to test individual elements. To save money, I often use a common color brochure if a brochure is called for.

In my opinion, it's imperative to test a wide range of offers. In my experience clients almost never test the parameters of lowest possible price and highest price that might be perceived as value. Clearly I'm talking about testing for products that require selling a large number of units to be practical.

It should be obvious that if you have a house list from which you can hope to get a volume of sales, that by itself would be economically satisfactory. Then this dry test could be done with far fewer names.

The mailing packages should always be created by different people and, in my opinion, preferably independently of one another. I strongly recommend the use of top freelance writers. It has been my experience that writers don't do a good job of testing against themselves, and I feel this is true even if different writers are employed in the same creative department.

In this latter case, there's always a creative chief who will inevitably put his own imprimatur on all packages. To repeat: I do not think the best packages for testing come out of a single source, be it an in-house creative department or an agency. That isn't to say that each of them can't create good packages; it just says they can't create multiple ones to test against themselves.

At my own agency, we used only the top tier of freelance writers. Less than 5% of acquisition copy was done by our own staff, even though our people were certainly well qualified. (You need only look at the success they later attained as freelancers.)

My comments won't gain me any friends at the agencies, but I submit: One need only look at the income the top freelancers earn to realize that the agencies or in-house departments can't afford to hire them on staff. Actually, a number of the major direct-marketing agencies do avail themselves of the freelance copywriters, and I applaud them. If you use the best copywriters, you shouldn't be able to predict accurately with any consistency which of several test packages will win. I've never known anyone who had such ability.

SOME OUTSTANDING WRITERS

This seems like a good place for me to name the writers I consider to be the best and who have been so important to my success. All these writers have had numbers of winning packages. I like to say, although I can't prove it, that together they probably create half the mail sent out by the national companies.

Dick Archer—Former creative head of Columbia House, now retired. He continues as a freelancer and has written a number of winning packages for my clients.

Hank Burnett—A great writer. A high-quality talent. A true gentleman.

Henry Cowen—"Mr. Sweepstakes," without peer.

Bob Fisler—Made a career as promotion chief at Time Inc. Now in retirement, he's executive vice president of Evergreen Advertising.

Bill Jayme—With Heikki Ratalahti (his art/design partner) he has had, I venture to say, more control packages than anyone.

Herschell Gordon Lewis—Particularly well known for collectibles but writes everything. (Recently wrote a winner for my newsletter.)

Tom McCormick—Does a particularly good job when a premium is included. Has done extensive fund-raising copy.

Harry Walsh—In my opinion, the best for merchandise and insurance, but he can sell anything.

Jack Walsh—A fine writer who is very easy to work with.

Linda Wells—A wonderful talent with many, many winning packages for my clients.

Todd Weintz—Created winning packages for many publishing companies. (Wrote the current control package for my newsletter.)

People constantly ask me which writer would be best for a particular product. With the few caveats outlined, I believe that all these talented writers can do a great job selling any product.

THE PHILOSOPHY OF TEST ANALYSIS

The subject of offers is discussed in detail elsewhere. I'm not going to discuss the possible tests of billing, conversions (second sales) and renewals, except to say that test results should never be measured piecemeal but only after the total series has been completed.

I urge you to be very careful in analyzing your test results and to distrust any answer that seems illogical. A great deal of bad testing is done, and an equal amount of bad analysis of results takes place. In analyzing results, be sure you project the results to lifetime value.

Keep two points constantly in mind: (1) Because of lack of available money, most test results we get are suspect because the size of our normal tests is too small. (2) The same test made at the same time in two flights with different keys can easily have a 15% difference in results. (If that doesn't scare you, it should.)

For years there has been an accepted (not by me) premise that an acceptable list test can be pyramided five times in the next usage. I deplore the use of such rules and put them in the same category as believing computer output is an end-all.

People in this industry are paid too well to hide behind such premises instead of using their experience, their intuition and their research in deciding whether a list makes sense, who the list owner is, how they obtain their names, and who else uses the list. I may well pyramid a list test 50 times or I may not go for more than a retest even though test results from both examples were equal. The difference will be what I know about each list and its suitability.

An interview with Stanley Marcus that appeared in the magazine *Inc.* is to the point. He decries the present status of retail selling, in which the computer has replaced the individual's instinct and concept, with the result that in a mall with three anchor stores, all three will be selling the same merchandise at the same price points dictated by the computer.

At the same time, the *Economist* published an article stating that after General Motors had spent $1.5 billion for the Saturn project, they came to realize that their future lay in building the kinds of cars their customers want.

Too many people hide behind the computer and are afraid to take risks. Reward comes from risks. We in the mail-marketing business are lucky, because with the ability to test everything the downside is limited.

Don't be afraid of failure. If you don't have failures, you clearly aren't trying hard enough.

ZIP ANALYSIS

The tree analysis developed by R. L. Polk Co., and its counterpart developed by the Alan Drey Co., are two of the most widely-used tools for making an analysis of responses by zip code with the goal of improving order response.

This form of analysis uses computer software which includes all the census demographics for each of the 38,000 zip codes.

The counts of a promotion mailing, are fed by zip code into the computer along with the total orders received, also by zip. The computer is asked to divide the total results from the mailing into two groups based on the most significant demographic factor, be it income, age, home ownership, children or whatever. Each split is then continued to be split on the basis of the next most significant demographic. This continues until the computer says there are no more significant factors.

The end results are known as "terminal groups." The terminal groups are then arranged according to response.

In the case of Yield House, the terminal groups of zips representing 75% of the orders had a response twice as good as the bottom 25%. This was truly a remarkable difference.

The exciting part of this is that the zips in the bottom

quarter represented two specific groups of people. In the first group were people who tended to live in zips where apartments predominated and in the other were those zips where more than 10% of heads of household were over 65. It was totally believable that these groups wouldn't be as likely to buy furniture as others, so we could suppress those zips from future mailings with great security.

I have been a frequent proponent of the use of the tree zip analysis and have successfully implemented it on a number of accounts—but not all accounts.

Over the years, I had many discussions with publishers about testing a sweepstakes. They often were sure that their "very special" readers wouldn't be interested. I always said, "It's not true. Everybody likes a free lunch."

On test this generally turned out to be true. Sweepstakes promotions were winners.

When I decided to try a tree zip analysis on the subscribers of *Contest News-Letter*, hoping to improve my promotion results, I found out how right I was. There was no demographic skew. On single-factor tables such as income, education or home ownership, using an index of 100 as average, the terminal groups of the analysis ran 92-108, whereas the normal single demographic tables for most publications or products ran 68-130.

Sweepstakes interest was truly flat across each of the demographic factors. No demographic group of people either liked or disliked sweepstakes with any significant difference from any other group.

Another form of zip analysis with which we've had some success, and which we're using extensively on our *University of California, Berkeley Wellness Letter*, is nothing more than a straight household-penetration analysis.

In a household-penetration analysis, the house list of buyers is fed into the computer by zip-code quantity. The computer calculates the penetration percentage of the households by zip code. These are then arranged in order of percent penetration, and in our case the zip codes are clustered in groups by deciles.

At the *Wellness Letter*, we've found that promotions mailed to the top 70% of zips show 30% improved results when compared to mailing all zip codes.

Both these methods are simple and inexpensive procedures and should be tested by all major mailers.

There are a number of firms selling other list-segmentation techniques. I've had very limited experience with two of these firms, but to date I'm not aware of better methods than the two described above.

MAILING PACKAGES

1. Format

There is no one perfect format. You have a choice of everything from postcard to self-mailers to closed-face personalized envelopes to standard window-envelope mail. (I've missed a few here, including boxes, tubes and telegrams.)

I've mailed them all successfully. Sizes? You can choose from postcard to 9"×12" in standard sizes, or use any size your mind can create. For economic efficiency I generally prefer 5 1/2"×7 1/2", 6"×9" or #10. I have had very few 9"×12" winners. On the other hand, as I've told you, for years I had a newsletter client whose product had no pictorial graphics or color, and the control package was 9"×12". They couldn't beat it.

In my 40 years of direct marketing I can only remember five or six self-mailers which were control packages. On the past record I resist even testing self-mailers.

When I assign a package to a copywriter I prefer not to inhibit his best effort by dictating format size. The exception to this is when I particularly want to test a particular format or size.

2. Envelopes

Envelopes can either be promotional in design

and color, and carry teaser copy, or be totally sterile.

If I'm dealing with a size other than a #10 or Monarch size, I prefer to use extra windows, color, design and teasers, whether singly or in combination. Those envelopes by their very size and shape are already promotional; so make them even more so.

Monarch or #10 envelopes may be either promotional or sterile. I have no absolute rule. In the past I've made speeches saying, "Envelopes have two sides. Make use of both of them." I've also been successful with sterile designs. The ultimate sterile design is the closed-face envelope. In my opinion the closed-face envelope is only practical when used in connection with one of the techniques that allow you to personalize the material inside the envelope in the same process as addressing the envelope.

Window envelopes are generally used because addressing the order card instead of the envelope lifts response. As discussed elsewhere, one of the trademarks of my mail has been to simulate the typewritten name of the signer of the letter over the corner card of the envelope. The idea is to make this look as though a secretary had added the name to the envelope on her typewriter.

3. Letters

The letter—which I believe is the most important ingredient of the package—can be any length. For most products I believe in four-page letters, but there's nothing wrong with six pages or more. I have seen as many as 20 pages, and I thought it was great. The longer you can keep someone reading your copy, the better your chance of selling him.

For magazines with great awareness levels, the postcard, with its short copy, has been efficient.

Letters done in booklet form are more cost-efficient than single sheets. I have not found that multiple single sheets, printed on one side, improve response.

First and foremost, letters must be interesting if you're going to get the recipient to continue reading. Some of the best very long letters currently used are those from the hard-money newsletters based on predictions about the economy. They're spellbinding.

Another current example of good, very long letters are those selling books in which an incredible number of bits and pieces from the book are quoted. Fascinating!

I'm not a copywriter but here is what Bob Fisler says about copy:

"If you want the reader to do something, you had better be prepared to make it clear (and quickly so!) what your product is going to do for him or her. Why now. Why it's better than others. Why the price is right. A letter has to sound human . . . look human . . . be human.

Any letter must look inviting . . . sound earnest . . . seem fair . . . and appear immediate. Break up the page. Give your letterhead a chance to look alert! Never send out a letter that looks like a brick wall. Vary the size of paragraphs."

I'd like to add: Be sure to use good margins so that the width of your type lines isn't too hard for the eye to handle easily.

Ed Mayer had three rules about copy. He said copy should detail benefits, benefits and benefits. Ed believed in the KISS formula—Keep It Simple, Stupid! Finally he said, "Tell them what you are going to tell them. Tell them. Tell them what you told them."

I agree totally: The only things in which the reader is interested are what your product is going to do for him and what you are going to do for him. What's the price, and why should he order it today?

4. Brochures

There's no single rule for having or not having brochures. I've successfully used full-color brochures for magazines, books and individual products. I have also used two-color, even one-color brochures to sell a wide range of products.

Perhaps even more significantly, I've sold travel and some lavishly illustrated magazines more successfully without brochures than with brochures in head-to-head tests.

I do resist so-called "bed sheet" (25"×34") brochures. They're expensive and ungainly to read. If I'm using a brochure and I have a discounted offer, I like to have a coupon on the brochure with a full-price offer—which by itself reinforces the special deal in the letter and order card.

5. Lift Letters

The use of a short second letter reinforcing the deal was, I believe, originated by Greystone Press. It was the famous, "Frankly I am puzzled". . . letter which expressed surprise that so few people would take advantage of a free offer. It was a terrific idea. Since then, though, the variations on the theme have strayed and strayed.

In my own experience I haven't had a lift letter be a winner in years.

6. Order Cards

In all my years of testing I recall very few pure tests of order-card designs or sizes, but I recall lots of tests of tokens and stickers. I use tokens or stickers frequently, and on head-to-head tests I can't remembers when their addition didn't pay off.

The contract copy on the order card should be as short and simple as possible. Design should get the offer across instantly when there's a special deal.

Guarantees are appropriate to the order card or stub, if there is a guarantee.

7. Reply Envelopes

I don't think the reply envelope is particularly important. There was a time when we thought color made a difference. In fact I can remember when pink was the color of first choice.

Whether to pay return postage is testable. The only product category I know that consistently pays return postage is new magazine subscriptions.

Fund raisers, particularly for political campaigns, often put stamps (multiple) on reply envelopes. Several times I've tried this device on products—unsuccessfully.

8. Buck Slips

A buck slip is a single piece of paper without folds.

The best use for a buck slip is to show an added benefit or a description and picture of a premium. Copy should be short. Headlines should be big and eye-catching.

OFFERS

Offers are at the very least the second most important ingredient of the mailing package—if not the most important. They're possibly superseded only by the lists.

The prime purpose of the offer is to induce the reader to order—and, most important, to order today. In successful direct mail we do best when we give the customer a reason for doing it now. There are all sorts of offers, but the best ones give a reason for not delaying.

Some fast opinions about the offer:

A sweepstakes is a bribe: a chance to win a big prize for making a Yes or No decision.

A premium is a bribe to say Yes now.

Promptness is often the best reason for giving the premium. A Yes-No request is pressure for a decision.

A reduced price is generally combined with action now.

A FREE first book has almost always been the best offer for a book continuity series.

The complimentary or free copy for magazines, the so-called "soft offer," is so successful that I know of only one magazine (*Money*) where a soft offer was the control and no longer is.

Two premiums, one of which is for promptness, are often economically superior to one premium.

The word "charter," when appropriate, is often magic for magazines.

Installment payments are a great aid to increasing orders.

When successful at the front end, nothing is better than open-end monthly or quarterly billing to a credit card. Longevity of purchasing will be increased. Inertia is a marvelous marketing tool.

Automatic shipping and billing are wonderful for annual books.

When deciding on offers to test, be guided by whether you have a one-shot or a repeated sale. Keep in mind, as stated elsewhere: The same product offered at different prices will result in the same dollars per thousand mailed, i.e., half price will result in twice as many orders as full price.

Credit ("bill me") will increase net orders by 50-100% and more.

For most products, department-store pricing will be better than even numbers—i.e., $9.95, not $10.00.

Price points have natural barriers—i.e., $9.95, $14.95, $19.95, $24.95, $29.95. Actually I've had almost no success with $24.95. I believe you should change a $24.95 product so you can sell it at $19.95 or add something to it and sell it at $29.95. If you can't add to it, and it's proprietary, you'll do better profit-wise selling it at $29.95.

In selling magazines, it's important to sell an initial subscription for a minimum term of eight months. A lesser term will have a negative impact on conversion.

Initial offers of two different terms will result in longer average sale but will reduce total orders by 10%.

A "keeper" premium—the customer keeps it whether he pays or cancels—is compelling.

Membership offers, where applicable, will result in higher conversions. In my experience, ten points higher.

"Limited" is a magic word on offers, whether referring to time or quantity.

ABOVE ALL, THE MORE BELIEVABLE THE REASONS FOR A DEAL, THE MORE SUCCESSFUL THE OFFER.

16
SWEEPSTAKES,
CONVERSIONS,
RENEWALS
AND
BILLING

SWEEPSTAKES

I mentioned in my discussion of *Redbook* that *Reader's Digest* invented lucky-number sweepstakes. This new concept of predrawn winners pulled 30% better than the original concept of having a drawing from those who entered.

When I first saw the *Digest* sweepstakes, the promotional possibilities excited me, and I jumped on its implementation, full speed ahead.

We recommended lucky-number sweepstakes to a number of clients and produced several very quickly. As far as I know, after the *Digest* we were the first to capitalize on the lucky-number concept.

The circulation manager of the *Reader's Digest* telephoned me and several of my clients, claiming the *Digest* owned the lucky-number concept and we couldn't legally use it.

In those early days of sweepstakes, we did extensive testing to find the best type of grand prize. Cash always turned out to be best, vacation homes were second and automobiles third. One conclusion we reached was that the grand prize should probably be equal to about half the total prize value.

Second houses and cars are easy to communicate in brochures. Travel, while a good prize, is much more difficult to illustrate.

Henry Cowen, a wonderful gentleman who headed the creative team at Publisher's Clearing House for many years (and since then has been one of the master freelance writers) is known as Mr. Sweepstakes. Henry, I believe, was responsible for the much-imitated multiple-entry order form. To increase response, Henry has become very adept at making it difficult to say "No" to one of his sweepstakes.

How good is Henry Cowen? I can tell you I personally paid him $25,000 for the creative work on a sweeps for my own periodical. I'm told his fees are higher now. I also know of at least one company that chose to pay him a royalty of $5 per thousand pieces mailed. They paid him well over $100,000.

Was he worth it? One indication: That same company bought a number of other sweeps from Henry over the years.

The sweepstakes Henry did for me was for *Contest News-Letter*. I know you've read statistics telling how much third-class mail is never delivered and when it is, perhaps 30% of the mail is not opened.

I have never held much store by this latter figure, as I believe mail for most people is like a ringing telephone and the curiosity of the recipients gets the better of them. The only type of mail likely to go unopened is mail the recipient believes he recognizes as something he has already seen and decided he isn't interested in. On a daily basis most people don't receive very many pieces of mail.

The prize structure for our sweepstakes for *Contest News-Letter* was very modest. A $10,000 first prize and five prizes of $1,000 each was the total structure. Analysis of a number of national sweepstakes had shown us that a $10,000 first prize would put us in the 70-percentile ranking of all sweepstakes. Over a period of eight months we mailed nine million pieces. We received a 25% Yes return, or 2,300,000 orders. The Nos amounted to at least that many and the mailing of one particular month produced a total Yes-No response of 70%. All this despite the fact that the recipient had to pay the postage on his entry.

Pay-up for *Contest News-Letter* was always low, but it was particularly low on this package. This would still have been acceptable except for the fact that the profitability of *Contest News-Letter* depended on list rental, and those huge response numbers diluted the quality of the list for rental purposes. That fact notwithstanding, the results were astounding. I doubt that had we offered to give away dollar bills, we would have received that response.

Overall, I must have been involved in some 200 sweepstakes. No more than five of them were unsuccessful.

AS A RULE OF THUMB, I EXPECT A SWEEPSTAKES TO IMPROVE RESULTS BY 50% OR MORE.

For many years I found no difference in the quality of orders received from sweepstakes. The pay-up on sweepstakes-generated orders was as good as for non-sweeps. They also renewed as well as non-sweeps.

Today quality of orders can't be taken for granted. There are many cases in which pay-up is poorer and renewals can also be poorer, but I don't know of anyone who has been using sweepstakes and has given them up completely.

One of the interesting clear-cut trends has been the tremendous difference in response to sweepstakes from sweepstakes-generated lists compared with lists not generated by sweepstakes. I know of one magazine where, ranking lists, using 100 as par, the non-sweepstakes-generated lists were at 80 and below. The sweepstakes-generated lists produced results at 120.

Mailing packages range in complexity from A to Z, from

the relatively simple packages of a *Travel and Leisure* magazine to the elaborate, multiple-piece package of Publisher's Clearing House. To my knowledge, there have been no head-to-head tests of the simple package vs. the elaborate package. One reason is that it's almost impossible to test both types of packages—simple and multiple-entry coupons—because of the legalities. Based on my experience and my views of results of similar magazines, I lean toward the simple package.

In my opinion, there are finite limits to mass-mail cost-per-thousand. I've had little successful experience with mass mail costing more than $350 per thousand. I do know of successes—Publisher's Clearing House, for example—but I myself have had none. I generally try to hold mailing costs below the $300 level.

I think successful sweepstakes mailers will agree that the first prize is all-important. I personally believe that close to half the total prize structure should be represented by the first prize. The drama and value of the first prize is much more important than the total value of the sweepstakes. Where possible, I like to have a grand prize which is dramatic and easily conveyed in words and art, with an alternative prize of cash. I don't think any prize is more desirable than cash, unless it's tax-free cash.

There are several schools of thought regarding the total number of prizes, the total number of layers of prizes, and whether all prizes should be offered with alternatives—this or that. In my opinion four layers of prizes are enough. The question of alternatives lies with the kind of prize structure as well as the type of people reached. Personally, I'm happy with a maximum of 1,000 prizes. Most times I'm content with substantially fewer than 500.

IN SWEEPSTAKES, SIMPLER IS BETTER

My preference for a simplified but dramatic prize structure stems from a belief that it's easier to convey a simple structure to the reader without the mailing appearing too busy and cluttered. I believe people enter sweepstakes to win the grand prize, not because there are quantities of consolation prizes.

I used sweepstakes in the renewal series of *Contest News-Letter*, and I was much more successful with a $1,000 single prize than I was with 100 watches worth a total of $3,000. I also successfully introduced mini-sweepstakes in the renewal series of some of my clients.

Copywriters have tried and tried, but I do not believe that anyone has bettered the lead, "You may already have won..."

A basic copy premise in selling by mail says that if you have a premium, then sell the premium and give away the product.

Nowhere is this more true than in sweepstakes. The premium, of course, is the numbered ticket, the entry form, the chance to win a prize. Copy for sweepstakes (our premium in this case) tends to be most of the mailing package, with very little said about the product.

In one case I know of, test-pyramiding was done three times, up to a final million-piece test. All tests clearly showed that an extra brochure, selling the editorial product, cost money and had no positive results. Actually the publisher's and the editor's egos couldn't stand this answer and the last I heard the brochure was still part of the mailing package.

The customer's sensitivity to prices frequently tends to be much lower when sweepstakes are used. The pitfall or trap in future promotions is: Should there be no sweepstakes, pricing is an entirely new ballgame.

CAREFUL WITH SWEEPSTAKES RULES!

In the early days of sweepstakes it was pretty much the rule to pay off only those prizes for which winning tickets were returned. This meant that, with 10-40% of addressees, returning entries, only, 10-40% of the prizes should have been awarded.

In actual fact, Congressional sweepstakes hearings compiled a tremendous amount of information showing that substantially fewer prizes were awarded than should have been merited by the percentages of entry. I don't believe this was deliberate on the part of the promoters; more probably it was human error in the fulfillment process, in identifying winning numbers among the entries.

After the Congressional hearings it was generally agreed to establish guidelines. Under these guidelines sweepstakes operators awarded all prizes by means of an extra drawing from all entries for the unclaimed prizes.

Recently, however, at least two major judging organizations have begun to permit the awarding of only the claimed prizes—provided that this is stated in the rules. Perhaps even more important, it had previously been construed that a sweepstakes couldn't test prizes of equal value to different groups of people. Again, *if it's spelled out in the rules,* this type of test is being allowed by at least one judging organization. I'm told the prizes don't even have to be of equal value.

This latter ruling can be vital to a company employing sweepstakes for multiple mailings to a house list. I'm not, repeat *not* making a recommendation. But, as I understand it, it is now possible to have one universe of numbers: Pick 100 winning numbers, then mail the same people at monthly intervals, selling the same or different products each time, utilizing a sweeps structure of 100 prizes; and have each monthly sweeps use a different 100 prizes, with each segment looking like a unique sweeps—as long as the rules indicate that different prizes may be offered at different times and that it's all one sweeps.

This means you could appear to have 12 different sweepstakes with a total of 1,200 prizes but actually have only 100 total possible winners and pay out only those prizes actually claimed, as long as the rules spell it out. In my opinion this is deceptive and shouldn't be allowed. I know I don't want to do it, even if it's legal.

THE ECONOMICS OF THE GAME

I'm sure you know that it's a common practice for publishers to use a sweeps prize structure for a year and get two or more mailings from it. A multiple magazine publisher might well use the same sweeps on all magazines all year long.

By doing this it's much easier to economically justify a prize structure of six figures and above. Some of the giant sweepstakes run over a period of two years or more.

My own preference is not to mail the same sweeps knowingly to the same person more than once. For the same product, utilizing the same list universe, I prefer to use two separate semiannual $50,000 sweeps to one annual $100,000 sweeps. I doubt that anyone has empirical knowledge, but I am satisfied with what I think I know. I do know I don't have to worry about being deceptive.

Perhaps I should say a word about economics. If you can (and I think you can) expect a sweepstakes to increase results by 50-100%, then it follows you can increase your mailing costs, including prize structure, by that much and still have the same net cost per order.

When I think about the cost of sweepstakes, I think in terms of $15-$20 per thousand for prizes and $15-$50 per thousand in mailing package costs. I consider that I'm not paying postage on the reply mail, as I would in a conventional package. This adds up to $30-$70 per thousand, which on an average $300 package becomes only a 7-23% increase in costs.

I previously mentioned the judging organizations. I urge you to use one. They can provide few services or many, according to your desires. At the very least they're up to date with what is legal and will keep you from breaking the law. They act as disinterested third parties and lend you authenticity. They pick your winners. They help you with prizes and prize structures. They actually handle checking entries for winning numbers, if you want them to.

Most important, judging organizations know the business. In the event you're interested, I use Marden-Kane of Lake Success, NY, as my judging organization.

THE MOST INNOVATIVE SWEEPSTAKES I'VE EVER SEEN

I think the most innovative sweepstakes concept I've ever seen was developed by SOHIO for its gas stations.

As I remember, SOHIO ran an individual sweepstakes for each gas station. The promotion ran for six weeks and each week 100 prizes were awarded. The big-volume prize was a set of steak knives and there were two or three bigger prizes weekly. At the end of the promotion period, there was a drawing for a color television from all the winners who had claimed their prizes in the weekly contests.

Copy for the promotion read, "You have a one out of three chance of being a winner." These odds were based on the fact that a mailing for a gasoline station's trading area ran to about 2,000. To make the promise of one out of three come true, the recipient had to visit the station each week to check whether he was one of the week's 100 winners.

The economics work. And look at the potential payoff: Who is going to check the winners at the station without buying gas? How many entrants will form a new gasoline buying pattern?

I've never had the opportunity to imitate this promotion, but I certainly would like to. The Polk Co. did several successful traffic-building "everybody wins" sweepstakes that resulted in a startlingly high percentage of recipients making store visits. The structure of these sweepstakes was built around an inexpensive bottom prize and several more attractive top prizes. As I remember, for at least one of them, some 40% of mail recipients visited the stores. (I believe this figure was for a chain of paint stores.)

Most marketers don't seem to grasp the dynamics of "everybody wins," which is nothing but a few added major prizes to a promotion that gives a premium to every entrant. The concept is particularly good for promoting store traffic.

I'm totally at a loss to understand why variations of these two successful sweepstakes ideas aren't widely used in retail marketing.

CONVERSIONS

"Conversion" is a term meaning a second sale of subscriptions in publishing. In two-step advertising, conversion is making a sale to an inquirer.

We pay particular attention to conversion in publishing because, as I said before, we know that a two-time buyer is roughly twice as likely to buy again as a one-time buyer.

Many times, depending on the amount of money involved, when the first sale or trial is sold at deep discount we price the second sale at a level between the first sale and full price. This is called a "step-up." There's no general rule for its success. It certainly is testworthy.

Considerable opinion backs the notion that subscriptions sold through Publisher's Clearing House and the other direct-mail agencies should be converted through the same offer originally generating the subscription by the agency. I've seen success in doing this; but in general I'm against it.

I prefer, if at all possible, to increase to full price on the second sale. I don't like postponement in getting full price. The results of any test of a reduced price on second sale should always be analyzed on the basis of profit from lifetime value.

A conversion (second sale) subscription sold at less than full price is not as likely to renew as the conversion sold at full price.

How many efforts you use in a renewal series is a question of economics, but in making that calculation you must keep in mind that there is a point at which the renewal buyer is not as good a customer for the next sale as a new customer—i.e., a telephone-sold conversion at expiration will probably cost as much as a new subscriber, but will renew at a much lower rate.

In two-step selling, in which people are asked to send for more information or a free catalog, it always amazes me what a poor job some mailers do of fulfilling the request and converting the inquiry to sale.

Numerous test reports have been made about response to information and free-catalog offers, always with the same overall miserable results showing how many companies failed to respond or how long it took many of them. It was always only a few who responded quickly with the information offered.

If I were responding to a request for information or a catalog, I'd want turnaround time to be 48 hours. I'd always put a billboard on the outside of the mailing piece advising the recipient that this was the information or catalog she had requested.

If you want to see a conversion series that is really done by professionals, respond to a Troybuilt Rototiller ad or any other Garden Way ad. They handle it very, very well. They've built a business of some $100 million with two-step advertising. Another excellent conversion series is the one by Warner Electric.

The good conversion series responds quickly and often, sometimes twice a week. It starts out congratulating you on being smart to want more information. Then the tone quickly changes: Why haven't you bought yet? You know you were so smart to inquire—but you haven't bought yet.

Perhaps the ultimate masters of two-step promotion are the insurance companies who offer you more information and a premium. The really smart salesman doesn't wait for a response. He telephones for an appointment to bring you the information and your premium.

Cataloguers, all of whom know the value of their house list and the extra value of a multiple buyer, do the least about conversion of one-time buyers to two-time buyers. There's no doubt in my mind: If catalogs acknowledged first orders with a special offer, a premium offer or a limited-time rebate check for goods from the same catalog within a short time, the technique would work very well.

Worse yet, regarding catalogs, those advertising individual items in general media do nothing special to remind the customer that he previously bought from the company or to thank him with a special offer on their current catalog. The catalogs generally ignore the need to do something special to convert the customer from having been a buyer of an item advertised in the *New Yorker,* or *Better Homes and Gardens* or wherever, to being a direct catalog customer.

How many people will remember the catalog's name? Instead they remember, "I bought it from an ad in *The New Yorker.*" The rule is:

A CUSTOMER WHO BUYS TWICE IS TWICE AS LIKELY TO BUY AGAIN AS A CUSTOMER WHO HAS BOUGHT ONCE, SO YOU SHOULD SPEND AS MUCH EXTRA EFFORT TO GET A CUSTOMER TO BUY TWICE AS YOU DID TO GET HIM OR HER TO BUY THE FIRST TIME.

In two-steps, if an inquiry costs $10, surely it should be worth another $10 to convert the inquiry to a sale. Conversion money should be spent quickly, while the customer is a hot prospect or is happily satisfied with his first purchase.

You can't afford not to test this. Jump on that inquiry and ask him to buy again and again and again. When someone buys the first time, from whatever source, treat that individual as someone special and get that second sale.

RENEWALS

DISCLAIMER: My views on renewals are mine alone. I know of no one who agrees with them.

With that understanding on the table, here are some quick Benson observations:

I don't believe copy and format of renewal efforts have any effect, assuming that the renewal series is adequate to start.

I believe the product, or, if you will, the editor, is responsible for renewals. After all, what is a copywriter going to say in a renewal letter to a customer dissatisfied with the editorial package?

I do believe timing counts.

The number of efforts is important.

First-class postage, instead of third-class, will of-

ten more than pay for itself in a renewal promotion. (I don't believe in paying reply postage for
renewals, although I understand Time Inc. has
recently gone back to using prepaid business reply
envelopes.)

Offers—i.e., premium and price, are important.

At *Psychology Today* we spent a ton of money to increase
renewals. A top freelance writer wrote the copy. Size of
package and graphics were varied throughout the series.
Postage was first class. Results weren't improved.

Actually, *Psychology Today* sold a very small number of
renewal subscriptions at full price throughout its first five
years, even though it reached a circulation of one million.
The magazine was difficult to read and not of interest to
most of the people the title attracted.

In 40 years of direct marketing, I've spent a great deal of
money on copy and format of renewal promotions and have
rarely seen an improvement to justify the expense.

As proof of my thesis that copy doesn't count, let me tell
you a story about renewals at our *Wellness Letter:*

I had decided to offer a free executive diary with renewal
if the subscriber signed a separate contract agreeing to
automatic shipment of the diary at a price of $11.95 in fu-
ture years.

I called my printer and asked him to pull the number-one
letter in our series. I dictated a postscript to be added,
describing the free diary offer.

But I had forgotten that this printer didn't handle our
renewal letters, only our billing letters. Instead of a first
renewal letter, subscribers received the first billing letter
with a P.S. about the diary offer.

We couldn't find any negative effect from using this
billing letter as a first renewal letter! Actually we had positive results compared to the norm.

Certainly this experience throws doubt on the importance of copy in a renewal series.

The Weekly Reader Book Club was an exception. A new
renewal series actually doubled renewals for them. This

was completely contrary to my feelings on the importance of copy to renewals. The new copy put guilt on the parents and effectively asked them to choose between being a good or bad parent.

"Renewals at Birth" seem generally to pull 5% returns, on average. A renewal at birth is an offer on a bill to a new subscriber, giving the subscriber a chance to tack on an additional term at the same bargain price or an even lower per-copy price.

I personally am not in favor of renewal at birth unless I have major problems making the rate-base and need every source I can get. I believe it's a mistake to put off getting the full per-copy price from the subscriber in the renewal or conversion series. If at all possible, I want full price beginning with the second sale.

Advance renewals are, I believe, the most underutilized promotion in the magazine business.

Advance renewals are, by my definition, renewals promoted prior to the regular renewal series. This isn't just adding a letter to the regular renewal series; rather it's an annual or semiannual effort to all subscribers not under promotion.

AS A RULE OF THUMB: BELIEVE ADVANCE RENEWALS ARE 50% INCREMENTAL—I.E. YOU WOULDN'T HAVE RECEIVED THOSE ORDERS IN THE NORMAL COURSE OF THE RENEWAL SERIES.

Unfortunately, magazines generally look at advance renewals only as a method of curing a cash-flow crisis. Russ Bernard, who was publisher of *Harper's*, came up with a wonderful advance-renewal innovation at a time when *Harper's* had little money for promotion. There was some advertising in the magazine, and in order to maintain the level of advertising, the rate-base needed to be held. Russ came up with the idea of an advance renewal at Christmastime, using as a premium a gift subscription at no extra cost.

If you can envision advance renewals pulling 10% or

more, you can better visualize what this can do for a magazine's rate-base with no additional circulation cost or circulation income. The basic effort is a renewal one. It pulls full-price renewals, which are 50% incremental and justify the cost of the promotion.

The extra bonus is that the gift subscriptions given as premiums will renew the following year at rates very comparable to other Christmas gifts. I've employed this technique with a number of magazines.

Another twist on advance renewals occurred at *Boardroom Reports.* An advance renewal offered a six-month subscription to a new newsletter as a premium. Results were the highest (more than 20%) I ever experienced, and conversion of the free subscription after six months was 20%.

In our own product, the *Wellness Letter,* last year (1986-87) we gave away an executive diary with a renewal. The customer, however, had to sign an order for automatic shipment in future years at an $11.95 price to qualify for the free diary.

Renewals improved enough to absorb half the cost of the free diary. The economic question will be answered in the second year, when we find out how many people pay for their new diary.

For many years I was a member of the board of directors of Historical Times, Inc. This story illustrates a potential problem for an advance renewal:

The board had reached the conclusion that our magazine *Early American Life* could no longer exist unless prices were raised, so the decision was made to do so. At that point the company's president took a sabbatical year off to go to England.

The publisher of *Early American Life* was instructed to raise prices and the board also agreed to put our subscriber list on the rental market to increase our income.

At our next board meeting the publisher proudly announced he had done an advance renewal mailing at the old prices and it had been so successful that he had sold an average of one-half year to the whole subscription list. This effectively delayed any effect of a price increase by six months.

Here's a side story to this: In addition, the publisher disagreed with renting the subscription list. He had dragged his feet, not putting the list on the market for rental. When I moved a motion that the publisher be reprimanded for ignoring the wishes of the board, I received no support. After all, we were all gentlemen... nobody understood when I resigned on the spot and refused ever again to become a member of that board.

Renewals lend themselves to the use of mini-sweepstakes. I have, for several different clients as well as my own *Contest News-Letter,* used a $1,000 sweepstakes in renewals. This is a one-prize sweepstakes but its power stems from the fact that the recipient's chances seem good because the sweeps drawing is limited to the Yes and No responses from subscribers whose subscriptions expire during the same month.

An alternative is to construct a sweeps using related products as prizes—i.e., 100 prizes: If you're a winner you have your choice of a circular saw or an electric drill. The involvement is that on the entry (order) card you have to indicate which one you want if you're a winner.

THESE OFFERS ARE ANOTHER ILLUSTRATION OF THE BENEFIT OF HAVING A BELIEVABLE SPECIAL DEAL.

The renewal percentages of membership tend to run higher than subscription renewals because of the difference in psychology when ordering. You order a subscription for a specific term; but you become a member (in your own mind) until you resign.

As a result we frequently substitute a billing series for a renewal series at the end of a membership term. In effect we say, "Your current year's dues are due." We don't ask you to renew. Just pay your dues.

I highly recommend the use of a billing series for renewing membership. The same psychology is true for newspapers. Psychologically we subscribe to newspapers on a "till forbid" basis although the order form doesn't say that and there is a specific term. You will note that the *Wall Street Journal* uses a billing series, not a renewal series.

Many magazines have tried to sell automatic renewals in their original sales-order forms. To my knowledge they've done so without success. The only breakthrough I know of is some success selling on an open-end basis billed quarterly to a bank card.

A renewal trap illustrated by *Newsweek* is the offer of a conversion for various terms including a term of less than one year. Such a term, with its proportionately reduced price, can result in some incremental conversions. But when the next sale (renewal) is made to these less-than-one-year people, they buy at the reduced percentage of first-time buyers, not the percentage expected of second-time buyers.

There may be a good reason for *Newsweek* to reach for these incremental conversion orders. Along with *Time*, *Newsweek* has enormous requirements for subscription numbers. Somehow, though, I doubt that this is the reason, because when I raised the issue they hadn't even looked at the lifetime value numbers; nor had they considered whether they were better off through the next sale.

Let me make an important point here. My experience has shown:

INITIAL SUBSCRIPTIONS SOLD FOR AN EIGHT-MONTH TERM AT HALF PRICE CONVERT AT ROUGHLY THE SAME PERCENTAGE AS FIRST-TIME SUBSCRIPTIONS SOLD AT FULL PRICE FOR ONE YEAR. AN INITIAL SALE OF A SEVEN-MONTH OR SHORTER SUBSCRIPTION WILL DEFINITELY HAVE A NEGATIVE IMPACT ON THE CONVERSION PERCENTAGE.

The reason, of course, is that the full collection process takes long enough to interfere with the conversion series.

BILLING

Again, I'm in the position of being a lone voice in believing that copy and format have little or nothing to do with the success of pay-up.

I believe pay-up is basically a perception of the value of the product. I don't believe in threatening suspension of the subscription. It seems to me this lets the fence-sitting subscriber off the hook by making him feel that if that's good enough for you, it's good enough for him.

In my opinion a bill is a bill is a bill and should be treated that way. You, the customer, said you would pay, so pay the bill. To show you what I mean, here is the copy we use at our *Wellness Letter* for the fifth and sixth billing letters:

(No. 5)

Dear Subscriber:

Did we make a mistake?

When you subscribed to our *Wellness Letter,* we accepted your word you would pay the bill.

Sincerely,

> *Rodney M. Friedman*
> *Editor*

(No. 6)

Dear Subscriber:

Please tell us yes or no.

Are you going to keep your word and pay for the

subscription to the *University of California, Berkeley Wellness Letter* which you ordered?

Sincerely,

Rodney M. Friedman
Editor

I don't pay reply postage for bill payments.

With the advent of the "soft offer" in magazine selling, many publishers chose to delay the first bill to new customers with the purpose of having it arrive at the time of the first issue. I'm aware of several tests, all of which proved conclusively that the first bill should be mailed as fast as possible. Our own testing went even further and indicated that delay of order entry from one weekly update to the next week had a materially negative impact on pay-up.

Another example of this is the increase in payment experienced by some promoters who use the telephone as a selling tool in getting out the first bill before sending the order to the fulfillment company. The customer wants to know as soon as possible that you have received his order and will send him the product he ordered.

Since attached mail has come into vogue, we've adopted its use in our own newsletter operations. This means that instead of sending bills separately by first-class mail, we send the bills with the copies of the newsletter and only have to pay second-class postage. Total pay-up is equal to the standard method of billing and, because of the postage difference, saves money.

Hearst is the only magazine publisher I know who has tested attached bills. This publisher also found total pay-up to be about equal to, although slower than, bills sent by standard first-class mail.

The R. L. Polk Co., which publishes the *Harvard Medical Letter*, found that an additional bill sent immediately upon receipt of order by first-class mail, in addition to attached bills with the newsletters, substantially increased pay-up.

When we adopted this technique for the *Wellness Letter,* our own results improved.

Now that so many magazines are mailing with a poly wrap, I believe they too should adopt attached billing or at the very least should add a bill mailed with the first issue of the magazine to their billing series.

AND IN CONCLUSION...

There are lots of rules—and opinions masquerading as rules—in this chapter. Use them as you see fit. I can only tell you: They work for me.

17
BEFORE
I
FORGET....

Now I've told you what I've learned in the past 40 years about the secrets of successful direct mail. I've shown you how I used these secrets in solving actual direct-mail marketing problems.

I propose to do as Ed Mayer (the best-ever teacher of direct mail) so often preached, and to tell you what I told you:

Successful direct mail is very simple.

First of all, you must know or at least estimate the lifetime value of a customer. This knowledge is the very foundation of how to proceed with direct mail. Even if you have to estimate some of the numbers, you can establish your bogey (highest permissible cost-per-acquisition for a new customer).

Once calculated, the bogey becomes the benchmark for everything else. It is quite simple to calculate profit-and-loss numbers on the bogey, to see what results you need from your mail to meet the break-even point.

After calculating the needed percentage of return, the first question to ask yourself is, "Do I think that's a reasonable expectation?" I'm regularly surprised at how few companies, considering new tests, go through this so-simple exercise.

For example, I remember an Amoco meeting in which we were told that 10% of the next year's budget was to be spent on a promotion campaign to get the public to come in and get an application for the Amoco Travel Club at the gas station. This was an extremely long shot (too much trouble) to expect economic results. Actual order cost was four to five times an acceptable rate. Failure was easily foreseeable.

Successful mail has to provide a reason for ordering today. Reasons can be price, premium, sweepstakes, or limited time or quantity. The more believable you make your offer, the more success you'll have.

Regarding price, I expect order percentages to be lifted so that orders are equal in dollars-per-thousand mailed by each reduction from full price—i.e., half price will produce twice as many orders as full price.

On a dollar-for-dollar basis, I expect premiums to be more cost-effective than a price discount—i.e., a premium costing $5 will lift response more than a $5 discount.

Premiums require much research, and the first rule is that they be desirable. They needn't relate to the product. Two premiums can be better than one. Promptness is the best reason for a premium.

I believe in premiums and generally prefer premiums that cater to greed rather than offering editorial reprints. I have no proof that greed premiums negatively affect renewals.

Copy rules haven't changed since I was at *Time* magazine 40 years ago. Copy should be believable, written to one person, and easy to read. It should spell out benefits, benefits and benefits. And I still believe in indented paragraphs and limited heavy blocks of copy.

Margins should be wide. Type should be elite face. Four- or six-page booklet-style letters are as effective as letters printed on individual sheets.

I like type in letters to be black (no red or blue paragraphs) with a blue signature. I don't like typeset headlines or an abundance of underlining. Letters should look like a friend sent them.

Most important:

Copy must be interesting.

There is no stronger word in copy than FREE.

Long copy is better than short copy.

The offer, or some part of it, should appear early in the letter.

Endorsements are effective if the recipient has little awareness of the product or selling company.

If a brochure is used, all salient facts should appear in both the brochure and the letter. The four-color process will pay for itself if it's appropriate to the product being sold.

Buck slips reselling premiums are very effective.

Order-card copy should be clear, complete, and as simple as possible. If there's a guarantee, it should appear on the order card.

Generally speaking, the larger the package, the higher the response—but not necessarily to a degree of cost-effectiveness.

Self-mailers are rarely effective.

The acquisition offer of sweepstakes, discounted price or premium only slightly affects the second sale. (This is contrary to accepted intelligence.)

It's easier to be cost-effective by increasing the cost-per-thousand than to reduce the cost-per-thousand.

Teasers on envelopes are generally viable. Number-10 and Monarch sterile envelopes are testworthy.

Lists, which are more important than copy or offers, are the most overlooked area of direct mail. List segmentation is vital, be it by zip code, demographic, or type of buyer within the list.

Sweepstakes will increase response (positive) by 50-100%.

Credit ("bill me") will increase response by 50-100%.

Labeled or imprinted order cards will lift response.

You cannot sell two products in the same mailing.

In my experience, lift letters do not increase response.

Involvement increases response—i.e., tokens, stickers, surveys, decals.

Department-store pricing is almost always better than round numbers.

Installment payments increase response.

An inside (better than to everybody else) offer to customers will increase response by more than the cost.

A follow-up mailing made two weeks after an original mailing will have a response of 50% of the original.

A two-time buyer is twice as likely to buy again as a one-time buyer. Spend some extra effort to ensure that a one-time buyer becomes a two-time buyer.

An initial test of a new product should test two or three packages, two to four offers and up to 20 lists, utilizing 150,000 pieces in all.

Prepublication results are 50-100% better than promotion results a year after publication.

I believe in the use of concept and dry tests.

Using the best copywriters available is the cheapest money you'll spend.

Any test idea you honestly believe can economically increase response is worth testing. The biggest failure in the practice of direct mail is the preponderance of preconceived mind-sets.

Almost without exception, at every company, the cost parameters for testing are too narrow—including testing price, premiums, lists, packages and cost-per-thousand of mail.

Pay-up and second sale (conversion) are products of customer satisfaction with your product or service.

You must be scrupulously honest in describing and selling your product, as well as in your dealings with the buyer.

I prefer to buy from outside sources all those things to which I don't add a unique quality.

I never knowingly buy a service or product in which the supplier fails to make a profit.

I must have good suppliers, and I prefer to build rapport with them as a continuing client and not as a buyer of one-time jobs.

A SALUTATION

I believe a major part of my success as a publisher is due to my excellent suppliers, with whom I have had a very long relationship.

They are:

Don Chase, owner of Tempographics in Carol Stream, IL, who has been my printer for ten years.

Frank Topper of Executive Mailing Services in Palos Hills, IL, which has been my lettershop for ten years.

Mal McClusky of List Services in Ridgewood, CT, who has been my list manager and exclusive list broker for the past ten years.

These are the people who have made it possible for me to operate by myself or, as now, with the aid of my daughter, Helen Mullen.

A FINAL WORD

Tell your customer the truth, tell your supplier the truth... and insist on the same from them.
Finally:
As I see it, the promoter's goal is to get prospects to raise their hands and say they're interested in what you have to sell.
The product must deliver satisfaction if the customer is going to pay for it and not return it. In the case of periodicals, editors cause pay-up and renewals.
I know of no better way to make money and have fun than being in direct mail. I never want to stop, and I most certainly will never retire.
If you were involved with so many wonderful people and having this much fun, would you?